THE ESSENTIAL GUIDE TO
Tap Dance

THE ESSENTIAL GUIDE TO
Tap Dance

DEREK HARTLEY

THE CROWOOD PRESS

First published in 2018 by
The Crowood Press Ltd
Ramsbury, Marlborough
Wiltshire SN8 2HR

www.crowood.com

British Library Cataloguing-in-Publication Data
A catalogue record for this book is available from the British Library.

ISBN 978 1 78500 389 9

Picture credits
Many thanks to James Jinn, Karen D. King and Malcolm Smith for providing illustrations.

Typeset by Jean Cussons Typesetting, Diss, Norfolk

Printed and bound in India by Parksons Graphics

CONTENTS

PREFACE

One of my favourite sayings goes like this:

I don't particularly like tap, but I love tap dance.

To be clear, 'tap' refers to the purely technical, often without attention to the music, and to the efforts of those on social media – the obsessive search for the 'next best way' to tap by those who think they have invented steps that were in fact invented a hundred years ago. And there is 'tap *dance*', where it all comes together both in sound as well as vision. This is where the technical skill is put to use, and rather like ballet or golf, it only gets interesting when it's being used fully, with affection for the music, the history of the genre, and the emotion it engenders. It is the intrinsic quality that evolves from hours of practising the technique, which in turn raises the question of 'nature' versus 'nurture': this means that tap dancing is undeniably fun to do, but as with any skill, the fun is in the work, and this is either God-given – natural – or learned through effort – nurture.

Tap dancing for a considerable length of time has its rewards. I have performed and choreographed thousands of routines – which is what a dance piece is called in old parlance – and still I love the tap... as long as it dances. Tap is a percussion instrument as well as a dance skill, which as such has to be gained through hard work and love for the subject. Tap dance is a joyful, creative and happy thing, a rhythmic experience and a fitness benefit. It has years of history to look back on and take reference from, and where rhythm and music come into play – and in the case of the Sydney Olympics in 2000, tap dancing too – the crowd is enthralled. Rhythm is a natural thing for almost all people on earth, and my whole life experience of tap dancing has been eminently positive. A dance that has its beginnings in 'the folk' has to be positive to survive.

For me, tap dance has often been my salvation through troubled times and uncertainty. No matter what else has happened, I always had tap dancing, and the shoes to do it with. My own personal career has spanned almost every area of the dancing world, and I feel almost that my tap shoe-clad feet tell me what to do, so that I only have to listen to music and they respond. I would refer to myself as an intuitive tap dancer, and rely on the feel and emotion of the music to *tell* me what to use from my own personal catalogue of steps.

'Steps' in this context is a strange word at times. A 'step' is a simple change of weight from one foot to the other; it's a small collection of elements put together to form one piece, and a much bigger combination using sets of these elementals. I like to think of this as a *vocabulary*, beginning with single letters, then forming short and simple sentences, into paragraphs, then into more complex sentences, into chapters and into a completed story. The idea is that the movements of my feet use a vocabulary, and I call this the 'addition' method – and it still seems to work.

As a teacher of the professional and the amateur I meet all ages and all levels of ability. The young professional may be found at one of the many performing arts colleges in many parts of the country, and the amateur *and* professional are found at a dance centre, usually situated in a city. In London, for example, there is the renowned Pineapple Dance Centre in Covent Garden, which opened in 1979; the centre near to Oxford Street is called Danceworks, and then there is the lesser known but wonderfully bohemian Dance Attic in Fulham Broadway.

These places are where you go to really *dance*, to learn from the teacher and not from the concept or the syllabus; you don't go to learn to dance hip hop, you go to experience that teacher's *way* with hip hop.

As regards individuals who have influenced me, there was a Hollywood dancer called Matt Mattox teaching at what was then the Dance Centre in Floral Street in Covent Garden – the dance community will know that revered name. This man danced from the early years of American dance in the theatre and then on film, and for me was Hollywood royalty. At that time Astaire and Kelly had hung up their shoes, but I thought I was doing quite well if I was in a class with *the* Matt Mattox! Similarly I would like to hope that I have influenced many young dancers, and especially those boys from a completely non-dance background, like my own.

Regarding my own style, I was always watching the films of Kelly and Astaire on television from when I was about eight or nine; I became interested in ballroom dancing, and went on to do competitions. I didn't realize for a while why I was motivated towards dancing and performing, but in my house my mum was always singing (and all her sisters too), and my father played bugle in the Boys Brigade marching bands. Later I learned that my great aunt was a performer on the Music Hall stage, and it became clear that I actually had a musical background, albeit a local one.

This all served to spur me on, and all I wanted to do was dance – and I began to wonder how I could turn this ballroom pastime into a professional career. I went on a holiday with my family and soon chatted to the choreographer of the shows at the resort. He watched me dance some Latin and ballroom, and advised me to get some classes in theatre dance in London. Then a week later he contacted me, and out of the blue and without any audition, he offered me my first-ever contract: a twenty-week contract for a summer season as a professional dancer!

There is a film called *A Chorus Line*, with music by Marvin Hamlisch and first performed in 1985. In the film is a dance number called 'I Can Do That'. It is a funny and fast tap dance number and the character's song is about him going along almost by accident to his sister's dance school and liking it so much he goes away thinking he can do the tap she is doing: just as I in my own way had accidentally fallen into dance as a 16 year old boy.

The connection to the famous film continues, because it was the then-Pineapple Agency that got me the wonderful job of dubbing the taps onto the 'I Can Do That' routine. When you next look at the film of that number it is me that you are hearing. I was to prove the perfect choice for that job because of my natural and intuitive ability with tap dance. I am the fortunate product of that nature/nurture thing and it is what has moved me ever since. In such a short time I had come a long way; from nowhere, to dubbing a film that still inspires the students I teach now.

I have now taught tap dance for a long time, and have always been driven to find a style of my own, rather than following something everybody else does. It made sense to me that there must surely be room for other ways of dance, outside the accepted ways of a set syllabus. Dancing is a hard enough game as it is, so why would I want to do the same as everyone else? So I thought I would go my own way, though obviously using the sort of elements that are common to tap dance all over the world.

The desire for a personal style has never left me. I think now that in my business it is actually the only way to go, if you want to be in it for any length of time. Training is good, but a personal stamp is even better, and actually I believe it is what you need.

But enough about me! Let us get started on this particular journey into the world of dance, and especially tap dance. I am sure you will find lots of good things about tap dance you have not read before, so read on and enjoy the following pages!

INTRODUCTION

The adjective 'essential' in the title to this book suggests character and depth, and these are features that I want to pursue in an effort to illustrate this quite brilliant dance genre. Tap dancing is nothing less than food for the soul, and the proof of this presents itself time and again, as I have seen over many years in my role as teacher, choreographer, producer and director of tap-dance shows in London and many other countries since I began dancing. People do indeed 'just love it'.

Tap is the dance that lasts a lifetime, and which can be taken up at any age or indeed at varying levels of fitness. It doesn't recognize any size or shape, or any financial circumstance, since it can be practised anywhere, in whatever studio or cellar or backyard or shop. It is a dance of the people, by the people, and one that has, like so many dances, come about from the early beginnings of popular dance. By that I mean it began its journey on the streets and in the houses and workplaces of the people themselves... it is a proper *social dance*.

Popular dances such as the Gavotte, the Viennese Waltz, the Charleston, Hully Gully, Mashed Potato and the Twist – and there have been hundreds of such dances since the early days of the ballroom in Europe – are merely the beginnings of the huge story of social dance, and in truth I don't know if there could be any other way for something such as dance to become popular. It has to be taken up and practised and perfected and, well, loved by everyone,

in order for it to endure either as a simple hobby or as a professional vocation.

The amateur dancer can be as accomplished as the professional in tap dance, such is its appeal, and it can easily be compared to 'Swing' dancing, currently so popular at many dance halls up and down the country. Tap has this sort of mass appeal because of the reasons stated above; however, it does possess something which no other dance possesses: specific shoes with metal plates on the toe and heel to make the sound!

No other dance style is performed with this metallic addition: tap exists entirely alone in its definition, the metal plates being literally the 'taps'. This sound aspect requires courage, and like any instrument, the practitioner has to realize there

Two pairs of Capezio tap shoes, only different in size. The built-up soles give weight and substance to the work.

will be an initial period of extended practice and dedicated repetition before it can achieve something like a status that is pleasing to the ear. And then there is the visual look to be added, which is a whole other aspect! So it's not only about the feet, though of course some styles focus entirely on that.

Tap is not an 'easy' dance, and requires an intelligence *in the ear* as well as the feet. Tap dance is cerebral, and because of this it will be ultimately satisfying and extremely kind to the soul when it is mastered. In essence it is an instrument, and every instrument if not practised will just sit in the corner waiting to be played. It is a musical thing, with a visual inclusion. It comes from within, and again, as with any instrument, it will find you, rather than the other way around. Once this happens, you can count yourself lucky indeed to have been found.

The main musical content in tap dancing is the *rhythm* content, and rhythm is a whole human story in its own right. Where does rhythm come from? Who began it? Why do we need to hear it, to use it, to copy it, to invent our own? And if we do indeed almost crave this rhythm, what better way to let it inhabit us than through the body itself, without the aid of an actual instrument, such as a guitar, a piano or a trumpet? *We* become the instrument in tap dancing: we are the listener, as well as the innovator and the doer. It is intensely satisfying and rewarding, and its history is our history, since social dance is like a personal record of all our lives.

Each decade we have lived has a marker in its social dance of the time, and these dances invoke in us feelings of our own personal history, and what we were doing at that time. For instance, where were you in the Rock and Roll years? Who were you seeing in the 1960s when the Twist was all the rage? Were you into Northern Soul dancing in the 1970s? In the 1990s you will also have had particular tunes from modern charts to shine a light on your existence; and as you read this, in whatever year, you will have personal connections to 'your' music.

Not for nothing has tap dancing survived for so long, and continues to entrance, entertain, amuse and satisfy. Many of us still marvel at the wonderful

Fred Astaire, and the amazing Nicholas Brothers on film. With social media all around us today we can now revel in the knowledge that there were many other historical tap-dancing figures that up to now we perhaps didn't know existed. Not everyone got into the Hollywood machine and was made famous, but it did produce the figures we can admire and be inspired by if we take up tap dance. Hollywood fed tap to the world, and we must be grateful.

WHY LEARN TO TAP DANCE?

Why we should learn to tap dance is a huge question, and one that has survived to this day. In my personal experience I can give many reasons why people learn to dance, and it has been my honour to have found such wonderful and sometimes completely unexpected people in tap classes.

Recently I have been looking at a couple of fascinating books written in the 1930s on learning to tap dance. They both offer a contrasting look into the learning ethos on dance in those days, and we can see upon reading them that it isn't much different today! I would like to give you a sample of each because they are wonderful products of their time.

The first is called *Tap Dancing in 12 Easy Lessons*, written by Rosalind Wade and published by Foulsham in London. Ms Wade was the director of the BBC's Dancing Daughters group, and the BBC came into being in about 1936, so it's safe to assume this book was published about then. Rosalind starts the book as follows:

The modern dance of today is the 'Tap Dance'; fortunately it is not difficult to learn … the essentials are an innate sense of rhythm, a natural aptitude, and infinite patience… First class instruction will quickly transform the amateur into a finished exponent… Many people fear that tap dancing may have a tendency to over develop the muscles. This is far from the case, for this dance tends to reduce the muscles and improves the shape of the ankles. Besides these benefits, it assists the student to acquire poise and symmetry of figure; muscle development is equalised and superfluous flesh is reduced.

It does not take much effort to see that this book is aimed entirely at women, and nowhere in the book is a man mentioned. All photographs are of the lady herself, and all are of legs showing the aforementioned slim ankles.

I simply cannot resist the last paragraph that Rosalind writes:

Clothes form a great factor in rehearsing. All garments should be of wool, light in weight, but elastic in texture, and should consist of woollen underwear, a jumper, shorts and stockings.

Phew! She must have always only been practising in winter!

The second book is called *Tap-Dancing Made Easy* by Isolde of 'Isolde and Alexis, the International Dancing Stars', published in 1936 by C. A. Pearson of London.

...There is no drudgery in learning anything as interesting as Tap Dancing... and though you may get hot and a little puffed..., you will find that Tap Dancing is one of the most healthy forms of exercise, especially in cold weather...

I have endeavoured to lead the pupil ... by easy stages to teach him mainly the elementary foundations so that he may be able to interpret the rhythm in his own way. It will come naturally for him.

Evidently this book is aimed at the man, as there are only photographs of a man dancing, albeit in an oversized-looking dinner suit and black bow tie!

This situation about the student is in stark contrast to today's classes, which consist of 98 per cent women with hardly a man to be seen. But Isolde does say that 'after learning these basic principles he will be able to interpret the rhythms in his own way'. Strangely, I say exactly the same in my classes

eighty years later: I ask that people dance it in their own way, but with my rhythms and the steps that I have taught them. Using shuffles, tap steps, pick-ups and ball change allows a myriad of rhythms to be created, and all teachers will use these basic things in different ways. From the same set of ingredients will come an untold number of dance 'cakes', if you see what I mean.

As in any profession, to succeed in it requires some kind of innate drive or wellspring, and this is not necessarily recognized by those who ride this wave at that time. Dancers are, by definition, the poor workhorses of any show, but who have trained like racehorses to be there. Only a distinctive and extreme passion can bring success from such hard work, and often for little reward.

Why, then, bother to learn to dance? Why learn to tap dance? The answer is 'soul', because dance is intimately connected to the soul of humanity and the folk of the world. Every society dances, as every society speaks; it is so natural and life-affirming that we simply take to it. If it's also fun to do, it will be fun to learn, and we will benefit the more for it.

Dancing in shoes that make a sound enhances the movements being executed and adds to the benefits; one could perhaps say that tap is jazz dance with sound. In the next section I will explore the connection of dance to sound and to work itself, since all tap dancing is pre-dated by people dancing in the workplace or in the street and on the land where people congregate. In this way steps and moves are seen and passed on, ensuring the development of a sort of vocabulary across the generations.

Dancing gives a body life, and learning to tap dance will honestly thrill you if you can reproduce with tap shoes all the bouncing rhythms you are always (if you are like me) hearing in your head. You may even, like Isolde says, find it quite easy! And that alone makes learning anything joyful.

Your profession or your path through life should only ever be followed if you find the work pleasurable, or at least of little effort. For example, successful professional footballers, golfers, accountants, carpenters or musicians who earn a living from their vocation will find it quite enjoyable, and also easy inasmuch as the effort is enjoyable and not overly difficult. Tap dancing is undeniably fun to do, but as with any skill, the fun is in the work. This is either God given (natural) or learned through effort (nurture). The fortunate ones are blessed with both of these.

The professional has the belief, commitment and the certain knowledge that he or she is going to be good enough to earn a living at this fun thing they call work. To be gifted in such a way is one thing, but to make it your life's meaning for a considerable length of time is quite another. So where does the line exist between the amateur and the professional?

From my own professional experience, the people who survive and continue in the entertainment business the longest are actors, followed by singers, and then dancers. I have known eighty-nine-year-old actors and eighty-eight-year-old singers, but very few dancers of great age. Of course, the body will dictate many of our decisions.

However, for the amateur or recreational performer it is all quite different. It is enjoyment versus constraint, own time versus company time, and leisure versus the pressure of getting the skill good enough to be taken on to be paid. The professional dancer must maintain a high level of fitness, since to be unfit will simply mean unemployment: if you don't show up, neither does the pay packet. Dancing, they say, is the best of all ways to fitness, better than running, swimming, gym or walking. It is the engagement of the mind as well as the body, the spiritual as well as the physical, the emotional as well as the technical. It is a skill in all senses of the word, and one which is an unmatchable natural 'high'.

As to the question 'why learn to tap dance', we can say that either it's because we may need this skill in our profession as a musical theatre artist, or we simply like the sight and sound of it when we have watched it. I have taught people who were forbidden by their family to tap dance when they were younger, and made to do only ballet – no doubt in the belief that this may have led to something more 'serious' in terms of dance. I have also met people who tell me that tap dance is their therapy,

who say they cannot *not* do it, that they have always dreamed of learning it... and many more reasons.

The reasons are honestly felt, and in particular I love to teach those who have discovered tap dance late in their life, who feel that now is their chance. Tap dance is a great leveller, and it seems almost anyone and everyone likes it, and many wish they could do it. I have talked with people who seriously regret having never learned to tap dance, and who wish they had learned to dance and had become a professional dancer instead of a lawyer or a local government officer.

Many years ago I taught a very grand lady of seventy-seven who couldn't do too much jumping around, but danced with great expression and had a glorious feel for rhythm. Another man of eighty-nine years old could still move very fast on his feet, and remembered steps from when he was twelve years old to show me. There have been many more.

Why learn to tap dance? Surely the real question is why not learn to tap dance? So now, let us look at exactly who *does* learn to tap dance.

ABOUT THE STUDENT

Let us look at the difference between the professional student of tap dance and the amateur or hobbyist tap dancer. Both of these should be taught differently, but in the same manner and with the same goal in mind. If tap dancing is to be fun, then it has to be taught in a light-hearted way. The difference will out depending on the student's desire to learn, which will decide his level of achievement. Of course, the teacher plays a major part, but as the saying goes, 'Nobody can teach you to dance – only you yourself can do that'.

Teachers can lead by example, but dancing is of your own body. Thus one student may say 'I love to dance' and just jumps about with abandon at parties, while another may say the same and be a classical ballet dancer: it's all a question of desire and level. The progression from amateur to professional status requires much more than just doing things more.

Dancing is beyond a look or a sound: it is a feeling,

an inward connection and an outpouring, a soulful expression, and it's the same for both sets of learner, amateur and professional. Training to dance for a living will be discussed later, but the desire to attain a level of excellence is a matter for every student.

Then there is the difference between tap styles. The syllabus style or regimented style is ideal for the young dancer learning from scratch, but adults would not necessarily like this because of its particular look, or because it involves the use of arms

A typical class set-up, with a total wall mirror the teacher can use in a reverse way: the students see the feet the right way round to copy, and the teacher sees the result without needing to constantly turn round.

and body alignment. An adult learner is focused on the feet and the sound, and does not always look forward to the arm moves. The professional, however, will have to follow the 'regimented' style if they are working in a chorus in a show.

One outstanding difference between tap dancing and other styles such as ballet dancing is that students of any age, size, shape or form can learn to tap dance. This dance genre is classless, it is not dependent on financial circumstance, and actually benefits those of more advanced years because of the rhythm aspect, which will probably be enhanced by age and experience. Open to almost everybody, all you really need is an ear for rhythm, two feet, and shoes that make a sound on the floor. It would be extremely difficult to continue ballet after the age of about fifty-five, but at this age tap dancing can actually begin! The only dance style that comes close to this is ballroom dancing, which is also both a recreation and a vocation.

With Rhythm Tap, for example, you don't need to leave the spot on the floor you are occupying, nor do you need add any set movement from the upper body. It is all and only about rhythm, and ideal for the late starter.

For the professional actor, singer or even the musician, tap dance is a perfect addition to their skills. For the office worker, librarian or boat builder

it is a wonderful way to break away from the norm. It is an unobtrusive and quietly attained skill that becomes a personal instrument and is always there to impress work colleagues or family – who all wish they could do it too! Tap dancing belongs to every one of us if we take the time to learn it.

So, the student is everybody, and he or she is part of 'the folk', descended from a rich history of dance. Whatever your nationality, music will move those feet. Dance is so allied to music that they may be considered intrinsically linked – indeed, some would say that to dance without music is to miss the point. Of course, one can dance to any soundtrack, and this is entirely down to the individual imagination: classical music or the sound of the sea lapping the shore, spoken poetry or the sound of a train on a track – it's all possible if one has the mind to do it.

There are exceptions, however, and a ballet dancer may find it hard to tap – which is not surprising since the two genres are almost completely opposite. The ballet dancer wants to be very much in the air and off the ground; the tapper loves the floor, which is his virtual drum. The ballet dancer strains to land silently and glide effortlessly; the tap dancer sees landing with a sound as a virtue. But these examples are pointers to the same thing, and that is discipline, in that dance is without doubt a learned skill, and without discipline there will always be doubt.

CHAPTER 1

THE HISTORY AND CULTURE OF TAP DANCE

The historical and social phenomenon of Jazz dance – which we will establish includes tap dance as the first jazz dance – is so wide reaching that Marshall and Stearns, authors of the greatly acclaimed *Jazz Dance: The Story of American Vernacular Dance*, published in 1968, reflected that: 'The subject is so vast that after six years of research, we gave up all idea of telling the whole story.' This is *the* book for the serious student of the dance, but especially of jazz dancing, and the authors map out the route from the very beginning of dancing to music in a jazz form – *see* following chapter.

In *The Book of Dance*, written in 1963, Agnes De Mille is quoted as saying: 'Since 1850 there has been little change in Europe. All further innovation comes from the United States, Cuba or South America, and all broke with previous tradition. Africa is the chief source of these new music innovations.'

In thinking about the beginning of the beat and what happened to it (and thus about rhythm), we can see that it has no connection to those latterly added European elements such as separating the toe and heel, as in ballet or Irish or Scottish dance, or in the carriage of the upper body in the waltz, for example. Rather the beginning of the beat has as its base a flat-footed and stamping essential, and it uses a gliding and a dragging element.

Most important is the propulsive rhythm of the African dancer and 'the uniquely racial rhythm of the Negro' (John Martin in *The Dance*, included by Marshall and Stearns). The African style brings a difference in its crouching, skipping, springing and jumping – hardly European in that era of the nineteenth century. Of course, the absolute addition and the revolutionary essential is in the fact that it is syncopated, whereby the use of stress on notes is freer and impulsive.

Syncopation is the start of tap dancing... adding the feet sounds to the fusing together of joyful clapping, shuffling and calling out to a rhythm that swings and has syncopation. This new wave had to travel from the nations of Africa, however, and there were various routes responsible at that time to facilitate its spread, not least the slave trade to America. Tap teacher Gerry Ames in his *The Book of Tap*, written in 1977, states what has since become common knowledge:

What we now recognise as American tap dancing had its beginning when the start of the slave trade in the new World brought about the first collision of European and African cultures. During the long sea voyage from Africa to the Americas, the newly captive slaves were brought up on deck to exercise and entertain the crew.

The Africans first applied their rhythms to European dances on the plantations. As on shipboard the white masters of the Old South made their plantation slaves perform for them ... (at which they used the... opportunity to parody the white folks' grand march of the Minuet). Later slave dances copied the stiff bodies and the flying feet of the Irish jig dancers from the North.

This rough and loose beginning gradually became more civilized and formalized as a thing to learn and enjoy, and therefore to spread. The early and great jazz musicians such as Duke Ellington, Eubie Blake and King Oliver would help this spread by their music, descended as they themselves were from the slave era. Around 1900 and beyond, this music was called 'blues', depicting the social circumstances of the African in the New World called America. Before this it was called 'Race' music. The words 'rhythm and blues' and then 'jazz' were natural progressions.

Moving forwards from this time to the late 1920s, the predominant jazz idiom was called 'Ragtime', previously 'Rag', because it was uneven and impromptu. In other words, ragged and 'in ragged time' became Ragtime, and an extremely popular and revolutionary music style was born. African American ragtime musicians such as Scott Joplin, Louis Armstrong and Fats Waller were among those who were influential at this time, and who influenced the tap dancers, too.

In the hot summers in the major cities such as New York, New Orleans and Chicago, it is not hard to imagine this fresh and vibrant sound pouring on to the streets through the thousands of open windows and forming the 'jazz age', with hundreds of performers, writers, singers and dancers travelling all over America. Clearly, jazz and tap grew up alongside each other on these streets and in hundreds of towns and cities, and still do so to this day, even though both have diversified radically since.

In other parts of the world other patterns of social and financial circumstance were also playing their part in the development of tap dance. In the harsh working conditions of the Yorkshire mill towns and the Lancashire cotton factories, the machinery in these workplaces and the sound of clogs on the feet of the workers themselves would help to instil this feeling of rhythm in the body of the individual. The sound of the dancer was emerging from diverse parts of the world, and from adversity itself a new dance of the folk was on the way.

A well worn pair of shoes, once moulded to the feet, gives the dancer confidence and a feeling of superiority in producing rhythms. He will feel he can go beyond thinking and just perform.

The jazz dancer of those times was the street performer, the itinerant who could move and gyrate enough to earn pennies and dimes thrown into his hat, just by foot sounds, hip movements and shaking! These dancers were called shoe dancers, not yet tap dancers, and would get away with having little sound from their feet by using the body itself. In this way of street popular expression, dancing was a sort of social glue that would help with all the problems that integration by so many cultures brought to the shores of the continent. The dancers would inevitably become more innovative, and everyone would steal steps and moves, which would also progress tap dance itself. When the taps were eventually added – by nailing coins to shoes, or just using the nail heads themselves – tap dance would be officially born.

The kind of music that is ideal for tap dancers in today's era is largely dependent on the dancer's own perception and their intrinsic feel for what they hear. We don't actually need music as such because percussion stands alone in the definition of music. To tap dance is to make music anyway, but perhaps what we do need to watch out for is *timing*. If we believe, as I do, that tap is the original jazz dance and is inextricably linked to this kind of music by its timing measures, phrasing and syncopation, then we have to admit that as timing exists in most jazz music, it is therefore probably best to tap to jazz.

As a teacher, I have learned that people love to know when a step or figure starts and when it finishes, as well as how it gets there! I am quite certain the best way to understand tap dance is when it makes use of music. For many, adding music to the learned technique is the final nail in the construction of the ship, because the joy lies in being able to combine what they are doing with what they are hearing. This togetherness of feeling is what we love to have in our dancing, and that is why in any show – whether in a class with children banging away, or in a super-charged number on the stage of a professional college – the sound of tap dancing to music is usually the winning combination.

It does not need to be straight jazz, but it benefits from the jazz-type structure of the 4/4, which forms the basis for most Western music we hear today in almost everything we listen to. Earlier I intimated that percussion is music for the soul and from the soul, and we only need a metronomic machine-like soundtrack to dance to; but it's the *structure* we are most comfortable with. I think it all stems from the human need for structure and form. The lovely predictability of the nursery rhyme is a perfect example of structure when it goes as follows (sing this to *Hickory Dickory Dock*, if you know that rhyme):

diddle de diddle de dah;

de dah de dah de dah:

de diddle de dah, de diddle de dah;

diddle de diddle de dah.

It has a roundness that helps, and we latch on to that fact. It helps us understand the rhythm and enjoy the syncopation and the cleverness of the mind that has conquered the coordination of head and feet. Now… that's tap dance!

So, is tap dance an American dance? Or a dance from all over the world? The truth is, it is both of these: a new dance formed in a New World from the Old World of Europe and beyond by the people of that Old World and beyond. What makes it American and thus unique is where it was formed: the clash of these cultures in the towns and cities and on the farms, which produced an entirely new thing. It is, of course, American but with far-ranging influences. Gerry Ames again in *The Book of Tap* states that:

Most ethnic folk dances contain elements that can be likened to tap, but tap dancing as we know it today is a uniquely American product…with identifiable roots in certain dances in Europe and Africa and, like many American creations, the result of a blending of cultures – a melting pot of old world tradition with new world imagination that is expressed out of American spirit.

The jazz era was 'new' and the fashions were all new, as were working practices and social mores after the ending of World War I, and excitement was everywhere – ideal for producing so much of everything. America still retains this exciting quality, and we think of the continent in this way a hundred years later, in dance and music certainly. It could be argued that nowhere else in the world could tap dance have been produced other than in that great continent.

THE TAP DANCERS WHO CONTINUE TO INSPIRE

Early tap dancing was to be found in early American touring shows such as the minstrel and travelling gilly shows, and even in the burlesque shows that were going all over the continent and to all kinds of venues. Of course, the country didn't possess

an exclusive to entertainment: in England and in some more advanced European countries, performers were working hard at a living either dancing or singing or in comedy. The term 'musical comedy', however, was a wholly American invention, later to be called 'musical theatre' and taught as such at many colleges today as a course of study.

Tap can obviously be referred to as comedy dancing, and only a century or so later did various practitioners attempt to dance tap in a serious or cerebral way to classical music or to a contemporary soundtrack. The most up-to-date dancers in contemporary times have come back to a jazz format as the music of choice to dance to. Even music of the hip hop styles has jazz as its base.

As jazz is over a hundred years old, so is tap dancing. Amongst the early tappers are Barney Fagan, an Irish clog dancer, Lew Dockstader, George

Synchronization takes many forms and adds greatly to the effect in performance.

Wilson and George Primrose, 'an early Fred Astaire', and the earliest 'Master Juba', William Henry Lane (1840s), as related by Ames. His book also argues that a dancer called Pat Rooney came up with two of tap dancing's famous steps, still in use and practised today: the 'Off to Buffalo' and the 'Falling Off a Log'. These dancers were the pioneers who would invent steps that would be seen and practised by other dancers and then performed by them; in turn they would be watched by other dancers and they would then practise them, and in so doing, pass them on.

In this way, and only in this way – since there were no teachers, no recording methods, no films to see and copy – would tap dancing be taken up and popularized. Such dancers included James Barton and Harland Dixon (of Doyle and Dixon, two Irish performers); George M. Cohan, the 'father of Broadway'; and the amazingly named King Rastus Brown, a leading light in the story of black tap dancing, who invented the somewhat elusively titled 'buck' dancing, but who was also the forerunner of the great and much loved syncopated rhythm jazz dancing style. Before this the rhythms were probably almost exclusively Irish in all the shows. Rastus Brown is also credited with the invention of the time step (*see* details later).

Great and everlasting names that still inspire all proper tap dancers are John Bubbles and Bill 'Bojangles' Robinson, both pioneering black tap dancers; and also the Nicholas Brothers, who were, and are, so revered to this day and especially amongst the hip hop dancers in the modern world of popular dance. Indeed, they could be considered to be the original 'break dancers' who could do extraordinary things with their feet and their bodies. I can use these wonderful artists of the dance to illustrate the culture from which it came.

The Irish contribution was major and everlasting, so I will mention here the famous George M. Cohan, and of course Gene Kelly – and the man who I think is still ahead of his time, Fred Astaire. Belonging with these are the two grand dames of the tap, Eleanor Powell and Ann Miller.

But I would like to begin with Mr Bubbles.

John Bubbles

It is said of John Bubbles that he was impossible to copy because his steps were so quick and unpredictable that nobody could do such a thing as steal what he was doing as he danced. That, of course, was the way all steps were popularized by the various white as well as black dance acts in the late 1920s and early 1930s.

Famous dancers at this time who survived long after Bubbles retired and passed on would say such wonderful things to illustrate his mastery: 'Bubbles has a casual approach…his nonchalant manner contradicts the things his feet are doing…you think he'll just stroll around the stage when presto, he'll toss off a burst of sight and sound that you just cannot believe.' (Rusty Frank); 'I could never steal a step from Bubbles – he never repeats. He's the greatest ad lib dancer in the world.' (Nick Castle).

Bubbles tired of the fast and clumsy tempo that the other dancers were doing, mixing their taps with other things such as eccentric moves and splits and kicks. Up until then the black dancers were either guilty of just a flat-footed and ambling style or a frantic jig style. Bubbles dropped the heels and clicked his toes and heels together to form new ideas with rhythm! He was the inventor of rhythm tap as it is known today, and his casual style, coupled with super fast taps with a blizzard of changes of beats and accents, proved to be a winner. Bubbles was the first dancer to do it all: rhythm, cool style, elegance, speed and dexterity, as well as being enormously creative and original.

These times witnessed segregation and exclu-

NOTE

Child acts were quite common in those times, and many would contain future famous performers such as James Cagney, George M. Cohan, and of course Fred and Adèle Astaire and the Kelly brothers, Gene and Fred.

> **NOTE**
>
> A 'class act', or a 'flash act', or even an 'eccentric act' were all common labels freely adopted by these entertainers, and the competition among them was always very keen.

sion for the black artist. It would take many years of struggle to gain respect in such as Hollywood and Broadway, but probably all that mattered for most was to be working at all in those tough times of never-ending touring, and hard and dirty conditions.

The Nicholas Brothers

One of the acts that began the end of the exclusion of black dancers in white venues was the brothers' act of Harold and Fayard Nicholas, two utterly charming black children of about seven and nine years old who would mesmerize the privileged white crowd they played to. The Cotton Club in New York had a whites-only audience, but they took these children to their hearts every time they appeared. In film, they were the only black artists who did not appear in a stereotypical costume or character such as a maid or a farmhand.

The Nicholas Brothers did things that would not be attempted today, simply because to do so would certainly risk extreme injury. Jumping down into the full splits from a height of more than three metres (roughly ten to twelve feet up) is bound to upset hips, knees and ankles, but was typical of the things some acts in those days had to do to become a success. They were called at that time a 'flash act', but they could really tap dance, too.

These acts were typical of the obsessive nature of the performers of those days. On the question of who does tap dance belong to, tap dancer Gregory Hines himself said on camera that it 'doesn't matter to me who was responsible for the invention of tap dance – black or white, African or Irish, it means

nothing to me. All I know is, they did a bunch of things then, so that I can do what I do now.' Hines was another in the long line of remarkable African American tap dancers.

Bill Robinson

Bill 'Mr Bojangles' Robinson was in the forefront of the movement that brought the whole of the entertainment industry of that era together, which meant black and white artists performing together on stage for the first time, in the theatres, in the clubs and on film.

Hollywood led the world in the film industry. Dance on film in the 1930s and 1940s was immense in its reach to the wider world, and dancing stars were the pioneers of a massive upswing in the change in popular culture. Bill Robinson recognized this, and understood that to get dance on film and loved by the population he had to be all things to all people.

His was strangely a sort of Irish style, being on the toes and with little arm movement. What made the difference is the rhythm of the black artist compared to the white artist. The white or European dancer is neater, with a flair for correctness and a carriage that is upright and correct, with beats that are similar to the folk dances and the quadrilles, jigs and reels of the old home country.

The typical black or African dancer had none of this at the time; he had the soul of the earth and the sounds of his ancestors' tribal drums in his past, and this would hasten the arrival of jazz. However, Bill Robinson had the carriage too, the personality, the neatness and precision, *and* the African's way with rhythm so that he stood alone in his interpretations of the dance. He became one of the few negro dancers who performed solo on the (white) leading Keith circuit.

In 1932 he went to Hollywood, and in 1935 began his series of films with the renowned Shirley Temple (he was now fifty-seven years old). He eventually made fourteen films in Hollywood, cementing his reputation as an accomplished black artist, as actor and dancer.

Bill Robinson actually changed the image of the black performer of those times, and his date of birth

25 May is the official International Tap Dance Day the world over. A fitting accolade.

George M. Cohan

George M. Cohan was a man of truly enormous ego and not a little talent, an Irish immigrant who knew no barriers to success. Known as the Father of Broadway, he was at the same time an actor, singer, dancer, writer, producer, director, theatre owner *and star* of all his own shows! By the end of his life he had produced no fewer than forty-three shows in New York!

He wrote literally hundreds of songs, a feat almost as prolific as the great Irving Berlin. Cohan could tap dance, but it was more that he had a certain style with his feet. His was a mix of eccentric and soft shoe dance, preferring a stiff-legged cakewalk style of dance – and he was, of course, white.

People such as Cohan invented Vaudeville almost single-handedly, doing tricks and daring routines that were spectacular at the time. Cagney's impersonation of Cohan in the film *Yankee Doodle Dandy* suited the impressive talents of this star performer, too. In one of the last scenes, Cagney leaves the office of the President and descends the long staircase doing a quite magnificent tap step known as 'winging'. He did this repeatedly down each step in turn... but without once looking down at his feet!

Fred Astaire

Frederick Austerlitz was from an immigrant family from Austria. He was the complete dancer, and not necessarily the best tap dancer. There have been other dancers who could out tap dance Astaire, but none, I believe, who could match his overall and overarching talent in dance, musicality, poise and sheer class, not to mention his range of ideas with props.

He could also dance many other styles, including ballroom, jazz and ballet, and if the scene then demanded that he sit at the piano or drums and play and sing, he could do that, too! He was also a unique interpreter of a song.

In the early days, from the mid-1920s to the 1930s, he and his sister Adele were loved and adored in

London as well as in the USA. They were regularly over in long-running shows in London's West End, and when they had another show written and prepared on Broadway, they went back home and did that one.

From this early beginning as one of a child duo on stage, Fred would go on to Hollywood and achieve enormous status in the golden era of the movie musical. Tap dance on film is tricky to accomplish and much tap dubbing became the norm; but what you see and hear is the man himself, dancing with great partners or with a drum kit, a golf club and a hat-rack. He was inventive and inspiring, and even the modern dancers and artists of his time were influenced by him.

There is nobody else in dance who has achieved this kind of status – except possibly the man who followed in the years of the Hollywood musical, Gene Kelly.

Gene Kelly

Twelve years separate Kelly from Astaire, and for a long time he was compared to him. He was also from an immigrant family – Irish, of course – but he was from a different sort of background, which helped to form his muscular style.

A dancing career was harder for Kelly than it was for Astaire. He struggled for years against the money men and Hollywood studio heads as a choreographer/dancer, singer and actor to get his ideas on to film, but this was partly due to the musical of the late 1940s/1950s losing popularity. Kelly's musicals such as *Singing in the Rain, It's Always Fair Weather, Summer Stock* and *An American in Paris* reflected the newer world of post-World War II America, just as Astaire's had after World War I. We can arguably conclude that from adversity sprang the desire to distract ourselves from the terrible years of destruction. Hollywood did indeed do its bit to inspire and comfort the world at war.

To begin with, the films in Kelly's time were made more and more in colour and helped him sell his ideas. The unheard of eleven-minute ballet section near the end of *An American in Paris* when he used the motif of famous French artists to great effect in

Evan Ruggiero showing us all how it's done! Style, dynamism, visual excitement and rhythm of a high standard. Nothing should hold you back! JAMES JINN

his choreography is testament to his vision and his tenacity. This visionary approach is what elevated him to the status of major talent. As a tap dancer, however, Gene Kelly was not in the same league as some of the dancers mentioned above, but his personality and sheer screen magnetism when he danced did far outweigh almost all others.

Astaire had no production headaches; he just danced sublimely. Kelly, in his way, was much more than Astaire, and he remains to this day a master of his craft in all areas; as singer, dancer, choreographer, actor, producer and director, Kelly has not been matched in the film industry. He was a true one-off.

Eleanor Powell

Gerry Ames says of Powell: 'She was perhaps the champion of women tappers in film; like Astaire, she succeeded in combining balletic style with very fast tap footwork. She could hold her own with any of the best male tap technicians, and was one of the few tap dancers to do all her own choreography.'

Her first teacher spotted that her ballet was getting in the way of her weight shifting the tap dance way; it is very different, and in fact in many ways is the opposite of ballet. He asked her to put on a belt with sandbags attached to keep her grounded. Amazingly this worked, and the essential attitude that is needed for the body to tap dance was imposed on her body. She then set about inventing her own steps and rhythms. She would become probably the best and fastest female tapper in history; she is on film doing things such as *eleven* pirouettes from a single preparation in her dancing!

In those days turning and spinning incessantly was quite the thing to do, and this amount would faze any of today's dancers, whether in tap or jazz or ballet; Astaire, for instance, never stopped turning! Ann Miller was another great turner with close to the floor footwork that is hard to interpret when watched on the screen.

Ann Miller

This immensely talented dancer was never billed as highly as Judy Garland or Rita Hayworth in her films, but she did make thirty-two of them. She was the first dancer to be recorded for speed, and she set the bar at eighteen beats per second with her tapping feet. That sounds like a phenomenal number of sounds between NOW and NOW, but set against the current world record officially recognized at thirty-eight taps per second, it does not sound quite so outlandish.

Ann Miller's tap-dance career on film can be seen in such titles as *Easter Parade*, *On The Town* and *Small Town Girl* where she excels at the kind of vibrant and quick tapping that thrilled audiences between the 1930s and the late 1950s.

As an interesting aside to this, I was once asked by the then Noel Edmonds Show of the 1980s if I could match the then current record of twenty-four beats per second, held by the great English tap dancer Roy Castle. I replied that I thought I could, but there was no way of knowing unless I had a machine to count the beats. However, the show's producers could not locate it; further, the family of Ross McWhirter, co-presenter of the *Record Breakers* programme that recorded Roy Castle doing the speed test refused permission to allow the 'old' record to be shown as well as the 'new' one being set by someone else. Ross McWhirter had subsequently been murdered by IRA terrorists, and his family vetoed any broadcasting of him from the time of his untimely death.

Peg Leg Bates

Throughout history people have witnessed amazing things from dancers, but none of them can possibly match the achievements of Peg Leg Bates, the great dancer of the single leg. Watch Bates dance on film and you will be mesmerized by what a single leg (the peg) with *just one sound* can do. The rhythms he creates are truly awe-inspiring, and his success was never about his disability: he was really tap dancing, and better than almost anyone around with two legs! He became an international success, and he considered himself fortunate that his dancing was so unconventional and unique that he was literally uncatchable and could not be copied.

Evan Ruggiero

At the time of writing (2017) twenty-six-year-old Evan is a very accomplished and popular dancer in New York. He also has one limb missing, but in the same way as the amazing Peg Leg Bates, he has a way with rhythm that charms and illuminates those who watch him.

He has a couple of 'pegs' that he can use, which produce just the one 'thump' sound on the floor whilst the other leg carries out the more complex task of using heels and toes. But what Evan can produce in terms of rhythm and uniqueness is beautiful to behold, and quite easily matches other two-legged tappers. He has great command of his skill, and dances in a manner and a style all his own.

CHAPTER 2

RHYTHM AND MUSIC

Where does rhythm come from? Who began it? Why do we need to hear it, to use it, to copy it, to invent our own? And if we do indeed almost crave this rhythm thing, what better way to let it inhabit us than through the body itself, without the aid of an actual instrument, such as a guitar, a piano or a trumpet? Quoting my earlier tap instructor, the wonderful Isolde gives the following insight:

Rhythm! A wonderful word if you consider it – a word full of romance. If this were not a tap dancing book, and you so eager to get on with the business, I might draw you into all sorts of musings on the wonderful rhythms around us!

We cannot talk about tap dance without talking about the musical style called 'jazz'. Jazz music is wholly American, but was born out of all the people who emigrated to America before the early 1900s, as the New World developed. Tap is the original jazz dance, and in fact all the jazz musicians and jazz orchestras establishing themselves at that time owe their existence to the tap dancer, because before the music came the person: the body and feet of the tap dancer.

Before anything else we should know a few facts about the body's own ability to produce sound. The first instrument belonging to all of us is the voice, followed by the body itself, which includes the hands, legs and feet. Beating the body or the legs with the hands, or beating the hands together to produce clapping gives us a very early instrument. These can easily be attributed to tribal and various celebratory activities of ancient nations throughout

time. Centuries after this, Europe would develop its own early body sounds – the Germans thigh slapping, the Irish shoe dancing, the English clog dancing and the Spanish Flamenco dancing.

Rhythm is another thing entirely. Geoffrey Gorer in *Africa Dances* (1949) states that: 'West Africans dance with a precision, a verve, an ingenuity that no other race can show.' Shouting and calling and clapping and stamping on the bare earth of ancient tribal African plains can easily be considered as the beginning of sound from the body accompanying dancing. Percussive sounds are what we are looking at here, and before shoes on floor there was bare feet on earth.

But it's the way with the beat that defines jazz, and the word '*swing*' is the key to this way. Swing can best be described perhaps as diverging from what came before in music, which was a classical, usually 3/4 time, belonging to the great composers of the Old World of Europe. In other words, waltz, in all its forms and speeds, was king. Swing has certain characteristics, dynamics and accents, and it can be counted. Usually it is over what is called a 4/4 time, which means four quarter notes in each bar – thus each count is a quarter of the whole.

The 'swing' element is essential to tap dance, because its natural accent is on the second of two sounds. If I can call this essential element a 'swing note' we can progress. If you think of a footstep walking, or a step going downstairs, or, of course, a heartbeat, the second sound is the accent: thus for walking it is on the toe after the heel, for descending a stair it is on the second sound of the heel after the toe, and for a heartbeat it has a sturdier sound on the second of a double sound. All these are of a

Rehearsing moves such as this cross-over takes time and patience, but is worth it when the time to perform comes round.

natural origin, and the four beats in a 4/4 bar can be counted thus: a1 a2 a3 a4.

It is a double sound, and is to be found in every one of the elemental sounds of tap dance: the shuffle, the tap step, the hop step, the ball change, and many others. This is further explained later after the basic techniques section of this book.

Above all, however, rhythm depends on something essential to its definition, and that is syncopation. This quality deserves a special mention here.

SYNCOPATION

To describe syncopation you would probably have to hear it first – and this would mean you would most likely feel it in your soul as you repeat its infectious quality and irresistible pull. Teaching all ages, as I have up to now, just playing music with a syncopated rhythm to a class will have them imitating its lively and interesting style with a foot step or a finger snap. Western music, and in particular jazz music, would not be jazz music at all without syncopation – indeed, it is what makes rhythm *rhythmic*: it is what defines it as rhythm. Otherwise we are left mainly with tempo.

First, here is a basic definition: syncopation is about musical *stress*: it is the act of stressing the part of the beat normally not stressed, the off beats in between the counts of 1 through to 4 or 8. The counts are obviously stressed because they are the tempo, but when we stress the 'and' or the 'a' between the counts, this is called syncopation. By adding stress to these off notes we add a brightness to the tempo.

An example would be: 1 and 2AND, and 4AND, and 6 and 7AND, where the AND is stressed (the off beat between the numbers). This gives our 'brightness' and makes for rhythm. Or you could say that 'anything other than the tempo will be a form of syncopation'. Even missing a count leaves the next count more exposed to this stress.

Stress might also describe what the composer feels in his head as he battles to get rhythms out and on to the music sheet. In writing the song 'Fascinating Rhythm' the prolific and wonderful composer George Gershwin must have known what it felt like to have this amazing and strangely unforgiving musical activity in his head all day long. His tune has an insistent quality and an urgency with its syncopations, and even in the title there is a hint of stress. If you know of this song you can read it with this attribute and see for yourself.

Fascinating rhythm (1 and 2 and 3AND...)
You got me on the go (a 5 and 6 and 7...)
Fascinating rhythm, I'm all a quiver (1and 2 and 3AND a 5 and 6AND)

Sing these words with the stress on the ANDs. Then carry on a little longer:

Each morning I wake up with the sun
Start a hopping, never stopping
Once it didn't matter, but now you're doing wrong
Won't you take a day off, decide to run along?
                        George Gershwin 1924

I can quite imagine him wishing sometimes to be free from the rhythm and able to relax. Gershwin was around at exactly the same time as Fred Astaire, and a more perfect meeting of minds is hard to imagine – one with the unique quality of urgency in the body, and one with the same quality in the head, a coincidence that we are still benefiting from today.

Quite possibly rhythm could drive a person crazy because of its excessive and incessant nature, and this is what the great Gershwin meant by that song. He wanted to achieve in the music the immediate and pulsating rhythm of the city of New York, and in those early days of post-World War I social culture, when all seemed fresh and new after the dark years, he succeeded. The words give the impression of being almost a slave to the rhythm.

Syncopation is *the* essential feature of music to dance to, and certainly to tap dance to. It is the loose and cheeky diversion from the essential but predictable restraint of the tempo we all must stick to; it is the fascinating thing on top of the base unit of time. It is actually why we tap dance. It is the unexpected and spontaneous accenting of the *off beat*.

WHICH MUSIC TO CHOOSE TO DANCE TO

I now want to briefly mention music structure, and what could be called the 'best' music to tap dance to. It is, of course, completely subjective, and mostly down to every dancer's personal preference. However, in my opinion the four beats to the bar format is the sound and solid base both for learning and dancing. As described above, the sounds on top of this established tempo are the syncopations, which are making the essential and actual rhythm.

I like to use a Latin beat because it gives a steady pulse and an interesting mix of brass, bass and guitar, and can usually be relied on to be interesting in the syncopation, too. Adding the tap dancer's own syncopations to those he hears, creates a double effect, with syncopations over the ones in the music already. In basic terms we can either follow and tap out the *same syncopations* the music is giving us, or we can *use our own* over the top. Of course, the skilled dancer or teacher will make use of both.

To teach these two ways in classes is best because one rhythm is there for all to hear and thus copy, and the other is our own invention and we can diversify to our heart's content, depending on the imagination of the teacher or choreographer, or the student. It is quite possibly more about the ears than the feet, and it helps enormously if one does have a feel for rhythm, however hard to define that is.

Another of my sayings is 'we all have rhythm, but in some of us it hides quite deep within'. I simply don't know if we all have a feel for rhythm or an affinity or whatever, because rhythm can be different in people of different cultures. I have no idea how the Japanese count their NOH dancing, or even if they do count it. In the end, it really is better to dance to what moves your feet. In fact, here we do defer to Western-centric music and rhythm.

A favourite music structure of the innovative teacher/dancer is 'stop time', where the music from the band introduces breaks of silence into the piece; this of course leaves the tap dancer free to put in his or her own little bit of syncopation. These breaks can be one or two, or more counts long, so our music bar could be reading in numbers thus: 1_ 3 4; _ 2 _ 4; or saying it thus: ONE, miss two, THREE, FOUR; miss one, TWO, miss three, FOUR. *Hearing the silence is the key to musicality*, and as a close friend of mine says, 'you have to leave spaces for the gaps'.

This is entirely down to the students' own interpretation, and this aspect of freedom is true jazz, in my opinion. Longer than stop time is a *tacet*, where a whole bar or more of music is either silent

Having multiple shoes might include ones for the ballroom floor, for the street, and for the classroom and teaching.

or is faintly supported by one or two instruments in order to keep time. Or there could be nothing at all in support! This means even more freedom for the tap dancer, who can then demonstrate even more dexterity and imagination in this silent 'break'. Often a tacet is marked by a single chord on the piano at count ONE, and then nothing else until the next ONE of the following bar.

In trying to find good examples of the above 'spaces' in the music and creating rhythm, I will name here two of my personal choices to assist in explanation. With the first idea of the actual rhythm in the music being the one to copy absolutely when tapping, try to find the track from the show CD of *City of Angels* called 'You're Nothing Without Me'. The introductory structure gives a clear lead and counts:

1 _ 3 _ 5(6) AND 8.

You see no count 6 because it is syncopated out, and this is a good example of this musical phrasing. The regular counts in the bar are our *base* upon which to construct the rhythm; rhythm is entirely up to the composer as they feel for themselves. Syncopation gives the music of jazz, and 4/4 a distinct lift and a brightness so it has a sort of skipping feeling. If we just followed the tempo we would have no variation, and we would be literally only marking time. Each instrument in a band will, and can, syncopate differently, because a trombone cannot be played in the same way as a piano. This is what makes jazz so universal and open to endless interpretation.

For the second choice of these stop time and tacet examples, try to find a track called 'Cute', popularized by Neil Hefti, where he gives a lot of freedom to the tap dancer and leaves whole bars of four or more counts entirely free from any support, except for the high hat or the snare on the drums. It should be easy to find these tracks for when you are tap dancing.

At the time of writing, jazz music is not as fashionable as it once was among the younger generation. Many younger dancers do not have the same affinity with the style as older dancers, and indeed reject it in some cases, not wanting to look or sound like their parents' generation! Rather, today's music is based on stronger and more electronically created bases, such as can be found in hip hop or garage style, or in other contemporary uses of rhythm. Tap dancing can take it, however, and it's a challenge to dance to anything with tap shoes on as long as you can hear it … or feel it. I always encourage dancers to practise to what moves their feet in their own home and on their own floor.

CHAPTER 3

THE LANGUAGE OF TAP DANCE

In my book *Teach Yourself Tap Dancing* I began the whole exercise by saying I was not sure it was possible to teach a sound and a movement using just the written word, but that I would try my best.

It is a challenge just to get across a dance medium that is almost entirely sound based via the written page. I have never really felt it was an easy thing to do, and there have been books before: what could I bring that would be different?

I have said from the outset that I believe music is a sort of language, and as such, must have a vocabulary. As tap dancing is an instrument that possesses a sound and can make music, it must follow that tap dance is a sort of language and needs a vocabulary. We need to decide what form that vocabulary takes. How do we get it across so that it becomes a learned thing, and a thing to be learned?

Tap, and much of dance, too, has for many years been written down and explained. Any number of syllabuses have been produced, and continue to be produced, both in the UK and other parts of the world. Some are international and some are not, but all have a method of structuring the whole dance in an effort to communicate. Dance in all its forms is communicative, trying to get across ideas and meanings. Of course, in social dance such as ballroom and popular dance done in clubs and so on, this communication is not overly relevant. These dances are purely personal and don't stray over to the communicative ideal until they are performed, and performed to an audience. Ballroom is both an amateur and a professional pursuit, one having no audience and the other having an audience or even judges in competition dancing. This is not to say that ballroom does not need the written language for the steps first: it decidedly does.

SYLLABUS VERSUS FREESTYLE

In tap dance, the syllabus is a great way to learn to do it initially, achieving as it does through constant repetition under instruction, the required level of competence over time. It uses techniques that have been handed down over decades, in some cases, to keep up a tradition of learning by rote, and the pursuit of a goal in the execution of the ideal of dancing. These structures begin with dancing at the baby level (some from eighteen months, but not on the exam spectrum, of course), and there are syllabus steps that begin at age five, and which do qualify under the exam system. The teacher who is well schooled in these methods will have gone through exhaustive years of training, and in time will achieve a level of competence considered by the particular dance association sufficient to enable her to teach others. (There are upwards of fifteen or more of these associations, each one having its own way of dancing: *see* below.)

Such teachers will teach what the association tells them to, though it will allow for some personal input somewhere along the line. However, this 'freestyle' element will inevitably be tinged with the syllabus, since it is probably all these teachers have known after twenty or so years of taking the syllabus road to success. In this way the syllabus is both friend and enemy in its seemingly formalized ethos, because it leads by example, requiring anybody taking the examinations to dance *only* in the syllabus way. Each dance association will claim that its way is the best, and each protects itself against all others in its regimented way forward.

The syllabus is amazingly useful, and some are undoubtedly better than others. There are upwards of fifteen or more of these associations, each one having its own way of dancing, and always in operation somewhere in the world. They have evolved through many years of agreement and disagreement, and poaching and copying similar to the early days of dance on the streets. People will learn, practise, dance and spread the word, and these things are taken up by any number of other people. Over time each syllabus will be improved and looked at afresh as younger dancers have influence, and newer steps and ideas are invented – though in truth, there are no more steps than there have ever been, only newer ways of doing them. In tap dance this is true.

Even so, the syllabus is guarded and enforced by the higher echelons within it, sometimes to the disadvantage of progress and the younger dancer coming along. The purpose of these associations is not only to teach people to dance and pass examinations, it is also, of course, about being a business. Therefore there is always competition, with each association claiming superiority. Ballet and more modern dancing (not always called jazz) are both highly structured, and arranged to suit all ages from very young to adult – there are even adult syllabus examinations within the association.

Ballet is revered by all ages because it possesses that certain mystique, and has survived on its international and ancient merits for almost three centuries. It thrives on its tradition, and this is its strength: the positions of the feet, arms, back and legs; and the strict routine of barre, centre floor, adage, allegro and free work. All this is almost sacrosanct, and any ballet class will have this as its basis and strength. These aspects are welcomed and cherished by the participants, and fully expected also. The teacher dare not diverge from this norm, and indeed this is why people go to ballet class. They demand the class stays this way, and its familiarity *is* the point. This remarkable heritage has seen ballet survive for many generations, and will continue for many more.

FORMALITY VERSUS FREEDOM OF EXPRESSION

Learning tap dancing in the early days of dance, and certainly in the UK, was regimented and structured in just such a way, and has led to its current state of being almost identical to ballet in its formality. But if tap is a jazz dance, then formality doesn't sit with it: jazz music is not taught, and it is not formalized into an exam system. Because of this, jazz music has retained its essential quality of freedom of expression, and with a spontaneity that only jazz has – indeed it must have. Jazz was always free and always in possession of a soul, whereas tap dance was long ago overly formalized by a few no doubt well-meaning individuals into a system in order to be taught, and to add to the business aspect of dance.

In the very early days of tap dance, however, when it was the first 'street' dance (a term adopted by almost all of today's freelance jazz teachers in search of an umbrella title), it was learned by people *from* people. In this way it managed to hold on to its very being – an expression of the spirit of free movement to music equally as free. Tap lost a lot of

Getting the class to follow exactly is the ideal way to learn and get results.

An example of shoe styles, in this case featuring the Capezio K360 built-up toe style and their tonal taps.

its soul in the years of trying to rigidly enforce the steps and angles of the ankles and the knees, the singularly awkward position of the ramrod straight back, the earnest look of the dancer as she or he attempted to infuse some kind of soul. Tap was taught as ballet was taught, and was then danced in the examination system as if it were a ballet piece! Contrived arm movements more suited to the feel and grandeur of ballet do not belong in tap dancing, and in my opinion contributed to the drop-out rate of boys in dance schools learning to tap.

All the syllabus systems seem better suited to girls, and this applies particularly in tap. Where an aggressive approach and an abandonment of form and structure evoke the earthy feel of real tap dancing, real street dancing, real emotion in the music of jazz, it benefits boys in particular. Boys in general tend to be noisy and boisterous, and if ever a dance genre suited a boy it is tap – though having to learn it in a fashion resembling ballet must seem to him a little misdirected. I am not aware of any taught jazz music technique, because it is surely a contradiction in terms. There are, however, many tap techniques and ballet techniques in the syllabus systems, and each one is the 'best' according to the association.

TECHNIQUE AND COMMUNICATION

Having a great technique can be for many dancers the whole point of learning to tap dance: for these, it is all that matters and an end in itself. Dancers can in this way become technique bound, and often cannot give the dance piece they are doing on stage enough true presentation or communication: technique for them is king. The associations demand ever more complication to somehow bring improvement, but succeed only in burying the whole point of a jazz dance under too much technique. Performing a technique on stage is not dancing, and we are talking here about tap *dancing*.

This is where the teacher comes in. They have to be a good communicator themselves, and must always remember that technique should only be a means to an end: the student should be so practised in the dance technique that he doesn't have to

think about it when actually dancing. Dame Margot Fonteyn asked none other than Fred Astaire himself why he was renowned for practising incessantly and demanding perfection in all his work on film, and his reply was that he practised and rehearsed the technique so much so that when he came to film it he didn't have to think how to do it, and could get on with the business of performing.

Not enough teachers are this artistically gifted, and it is the fault of the syllabus not to encourage this artistic aspect, preferring, it seems, to invent more and more qualifications in order to generate more business from the parents of the children in classes. That said, there has to be a set of rudiments in anything, and especially in a physical pursuit such as a sport or a dance. Technique, of course, is the way to go, and in general the associations have got it right: there must be some kind of technique, or learning cannot take place – but what counts is the way it is taught.

Personally I have always been in love with the freedom of expression that tap gives, and have therefore not been too drawn to the syllabus way of learning, though at the same time recognizing its importance and the fact that we have to at least begin with a structure. When I was about seventeen years old I wanted to learn to do the tap I saw on the television – that of Gene Kelly and similar dancers. My teacher was 'old school' and taught the ways of the 'Lancashire Lads' of the clog dancing era, a famous all male pre-First World War dancing act of the Old Time Music Hall days. Not surprisingly I was unimpressed, and determined that I would seek out this other, much more attractive style of tap dancing I had seen on TV. This tap dancing on film was to impress me from that time forward.

CHAPTER 4

IMPROVISATION VERSUS CHOREOGRAPHY

True improvisation (or improv.) is in fact not really possible for the practised tap dancer, for he or she uses all they know already but in spontaneous ways – that is, without thinking about it. Thought is obviously playing a major part, otherwise the feet stand still, but the putting together of elements previously learned is what makes for improvisation. All the experience from all the dances and dancing already done with one's body feeds into a so-called improvised performance, and if improv. has a definition, it is that it is 'not repeatable' if you are going to call it pure improv.

Tap in improvisation is like jazz in improvisation, where the musician will call upon all of his learned experience to form a new experience, which he cannot repeat if it is to be that pure state. Having reached that level of competence the dancer can endlessly make up and construct a fresh piece, which will be improvised, but not entirely. Removing him or herself from the thought process, if that is possible, will give the dancer that keen edge and let the music 'decide' the steps. That's real improv., and can be achieved. Calling it 'muscle memory' is to give it a slight term, for it is more than just this: I think this is the way the tap dancer can become as quick as possible, in bypassing the thought completely.

THE RHYTHM TAPPER

The style that lends itself to improvisation is called 'rhythm tap', which, as the title suggests, relies on nothing but the feet to create the rhythm, with

The teacher's choice of music is important, since all open classes will have an age range, and the music must try to appeal to all those ages, to generate and maintain interest.

OK, now one more time. And this time on time!

very little reference to the upper body – the rhythm tapper will deliberately try merely to hover above his feet with the arms either hanging or gesticulating in a free fashion.

In my own classes I do a kind of improvisation, and then I teach what I have just 'taught' myself by doodling along to the music and seeing what arrives at the feet. In this way I try to remove myself from any thought process and just let the music decide – and it works (most of the time...). The dance piece itself is a new creation and it has been put together in my own way, so therefore I can hopefully say it is an improvised piece. Improvisation, then, is not as new as those who practise it exclusively make it out to be. It is tempting, and would be wonderful, if we could invent steps, but in truth all 'steps' or elements have already been invented: there are only new ways of executing them. Thus a shuffle can be done in different ways, but it is still a shuffle.

Even something as advanced as a 'wing' still has to actually *wing*. The foot action is a kind of a flapping action in the ankle on the return from the

outward stroke (I will try to give a better description in the later chapters on advanced technique). Rusty Frank in the glossary of her book *Tap – The Greatest Tap Dance Stars and Their Stories*, describes a 'wing' as referring to the action of the *arms* – but I am not convinced. Rusty is somewhat of a connoisseur, so she may be perfectly correct in her description. I will have to ask her.

One of the world's most amazing tap dancers, currently and for the past twenty or so years, goes by the name of Savion Glover. Savion is one of the quickest 'non thinkers' in the business, and most probably has never once repeated anything he has done on stage or film, such is his command. He is first and foremost *about the rhythm*, with scant attention to the look of the upper body or to what it's saying, preferring instead to be at one with the instruments in the band on stage.

It is possible to see that he does not need to think before he dances, and that if he did, it could perhaps spoil the true and raw nature of what he is doing. His dancing is about the removal of self to gain complete and instant connection of mind and body – and in his case, surely spirit, too. Such a virtuoso can also 'blind' the audience with the intensity being produced, and it is so all-consuming that both artist and audience can become lost in the fierce tempo and complexity of the rhythms. The upper body language is certainly lost in Savion, but this is his way with tap dance, and totally unique.

The good thing about the rhythm tapper is that he or she can never be 'wrong': they are just communicating, as we all do. The spontaneity of this style is the gift it carries, as long as it seems to make rhythmic sense. Of course, one person's sense is another's 'non' sense, so the rhythm tapper can impress with whatever comes from his shoes – but on the whole an appreciative audience will recognize the 'good' rhythm from the not so good, and react accordingly. Nevertheless it is a greatly subjective point of view.

This is all par for the rhythm tappers, but I feel that the whole body should tap dance: I think an audience does need to look at something, if only because it is not privy to the artist's own innate forces and cannot be expected to be as immersed in the art as the dancer is – they are probably not the purist that he or she is. In this sort of tap dancing the tapper is on another plane and almost detached from the floor, whilst the feet are free to go as crazy as they want to. Can rhythm tap therefore be seen as selfish? Can such a thing as a personal feeling be taught? Or is it like jazz, a product of learned elements now 'forgotten' within the body and allowed to escape through the shoes?

Speaking personally, I like to play with the genre because, as with ballet, I have always believed it can have a narrative, or it can just *be*. Forty years or more have given me a massive vocabulary from which to choose and thus improvise – though it wasn't always like that this: many years ago I came across a different language from a lady called Joy Adams. As soon as I walked into her studio and saw her dance I realized I had at last found the kind of tap dancing I had been looking for since I was seventeen years old.

Joy had her own way and language for tap dance, and it was because she was taught by a man called Buddy Bradley and thus took it forward, as all great tap dancers did. Bradley was the African American dancer who taught dancers such as Britain's Bruce Forsyth and Roy Castle; he came over from America at the invitation of the great Noel Coward, who brought him to London to teach the white English dancer how to 'tap dance properly' in his shows running in London's West End; it was fortunate that he stayed to teach for years afterwards.

Before Buddy and the style known as rhythm tap came along, the English dancers were merrily clogging away without that syncopation that denotes and defines tap dance. Incessant practice was Buddy's watchword, and learning in this way makes it easier to get up in front of a class of, say, thirty people and just relax and let the music do the dancing. Improvisation is a state, and it does not always have to be right, whatever that means. What the improvisation and rhythm tap dancers usually shy away from is a tap dance routine of length, preferring instead to just hang loose and, well..., make rhythm.

In truth, all classes are mini choreographies, since this is generally what the amateur dancer wants to learn; it is for some, the whole point of the class. The best classes usually contain instances of different styles in their construction; there will be some show style, some close footwork style, some rhythm style and so on.

Tap dance routines are arrived at through experience and practice of all the many elemental things teachers have been doing for years, but the dance piece itself will be new, arrived at by this process of trial and (much) error. Once a class of people understands this way of thinking – that a tap piece in class is a short story of beginning, middle and end, and thus a sort of narrative – it is safe to say a language has been used in the telling. It becomes relatively easy to learn and then execute a dance because many of the elements have been learned beforehand; everyone understands the process and the way of the teacher, and, perhaps more importantly, many of the actual steps have names. For instance, from these short sentences we can understand: *two shuffles on the right, spring on to that*, *do a single shuffle step on the left and a cramp roll on the right foot*. Most practised tap dancers will know instantly what is meant, and will follow the instructions exactly.

As with any physical activity, practice makes perfect, and as in sport or music, this practice or repetition is designed to improve the connection between brain and body, and is the only route to the performance. In this way a tap dance class will be following the path to getting better, and so will enjoy their hobby or leisure activity much more. Classes are not just about the end product of the routine, of course, but in my experience this aspect is really sought after and valued. It is why people give their time to themselves, and in this case gain the joy that is tap dancing.

CHOREOGRAPHY

All classes of all kinds of dance are choreographed or led by the teacher; even in improvisation tap classes there is an element of teach and follow. Choreography must have a direction, a purpose or

Checking alignment produces great results and justifies the practice.

an intention, as well as a conclusion, for it to be a whole. Even in the style of dance known as 'contemporary', pieces start somewhere and finish somewhere; they also tell a story, even if the story is in the abstract. Tap dance can also be abstracted, but if it's a performance it has to bear the consequences if the audience doesn't enjoy that aspect.

Some may say that abstracted tap dance isn't really doing the job of traditional tap dancing, using a balanced way with rhythm and with the jazz format and accompanying dynamics. Many people appreciate the *complexity* of the dance itself as the performance, and for some, music is not a necessity. However, predominantly it is the age-old jazz format and the 4/4 structure that finds the most appreciative audience.

Tap dance is known as the first jazz dance, and certainly it is the first *street* dance. Not until many years had passed did tap dance accept the constraints of the dance director (the title of choreographer came later; it was always 'dance director' on film and on stage), and it was the Hollywood of the so-called 'golden era' in the 1930s and 1940s, and the mass output of the film musical of that time, which established this new brand of director and spread the word that was dance.

In the early days of dance on film we perhaps recognize the name of Busby Berkeley and Agnes de Mille, who were the contemporaries of George Balanchine (ballet) and Jack Cole, the real 'father of jazz dance'. Tap dance choreographers would come along later, but at first the acts such as the Nicholas Brothers and the Berry Brothers appearing in a movie would just do their own perfected routines *and as themselves*.

It was common for the stars to do their own choreography, and especially in tap dancing: there was nobody else around who could set the sort of tap the stars were doing, and in any case, the whole point of these films was to see the stars performing their own work. They were in the films as guests, and usually played no part in the actual plot. Any chorus work was done by as yet unknown choreographers, but under the control of the director of the film.

Berkeley was the dance director who adopted the title, and his ensemble work in the famous black and white movies we sometimes see on television are often full of tap dancing. He could not set the taps, but still, *Forty Second Street* (sometimes written as *42nd St*) is the most obvious one that comes to mind. This was part of a run of tap on film with him as dance director, with titles such as *Gold Diggers of 1933*, *Gold Diggers of 1935* and *Babes on Broadway in 1941*. The choreographer who set the taps would be hard to locate, but the dance director was Busby Berkeley.

Broadway Melody of 1940 starred Fred Astaire and Eleanor Powell and was, and still is, the epitome of super fast and incredible taps on wonderful floors and to great (jazz) music. The choreographers were Astaire and Powell themselves, but the director was Norman Taurog, who would have staged the chorus tap dancing. It was really Astaire who first used and established the services of a dedicated choreographer in tap on film, and his name was Hermes Pan. Unusually, Pan looked just like Fred and he was to choreograph him for over thirty years, getting into the man's body and feet to almost become another Astaire.

The huge numbers put on to these magnificent and gigantic sound stages in the 1930s and 1940s still excite when seen today, but could not be repeated because of the cost in today's film-making world. Dancers would be put to work for long hours under terribly hot lighting conditions – but because it was a Hollywood film they were reportedly happy just to be on the film with Astaire or Kelly or Rita Haywood as the stars.

Tap dance choreographers (good ones) are quite rare, and in the past, few are credited on the films. Rusty Frank in her book *Tap!* mentions Louis da Pron who inspired her, and who was that rare thing: a contracted choreographer to a major studio, in this case Universal Pictures. Another contracted dancer/choreographer deserving of note was Jack Cole, who would give Marilyn Monroe her famous femininity in such films as *Gentlemen Prefer Blondes* and *Let's Make Love*.

Jack Cole was influenced by tap dance, but as with Bob Fosse later, he used the undeniable American way with rhythm and steps to get the results he achieved. Although he did not tap dance on film, Fosse would work with the idea of tap in his dancing and choreography. Jack Cole was a true master of the genre of jazz dancing, and was successful in Hollywood and on stage in the nightclubs so prevalent in those times in Los Angeles (*see* the biography *Unsung Genius* by Glenn Loney 1984).

Choreographing a tap dance piece requires a certain mind – and probably a frenetic sort of mind, too! As with drummers, tappers are that breed of person who loves the incredible detail that tap dancing has to have. As with any performed musical piece on an instrument, the notation is there to be followed strictly to the letter, and to veer away from this in, say, a symphony with everyone playing (literally) their part is unthinkable.

This is the very opposite of improvisation, *but* can have lots of rhythm tap and improv. elements if the choreographer has the intelligence to use these aspects. Far too often standardized steps from standardized syllabuses are copied into a performance, which is the equivalent of putting exercises on stage. The true tap dancer will be able to use the exercises, of course, but will not reproduce them slavishly in the dance piece: he or she will vary the elements so much that they are almost unrecognizable.

This is the choreographer's job, and it depends almost entirely on him or her having *musicality*. In a performance this is essential, and not all dance artists have this. It requires them to have a range of choices, which are then used to construct the whole, and it is down entirely to the way the music is perceived and acted upon. It is a personal choice, but one which is then put into another person's shoes (the dancer's) or into their head. Communicating the idea of the work is the trick *and* the task, and it will always require musicality.

Musicality

This again calls into question the 'nature versus nurture' argument. We are talking here of tap dance, which is a specifically Western-centric dance, and very specifically an American dance: tap is wholly American. Of course, in the New World, which America became around the time of the 1830s to the people of old Europe, it would be the people of these lands who would eventually propagate this dance form. They brought their own cultural histories, and with them their own folk dance traditions, which would lead to the mix of dance flavours that would eventually be called tap dancing. Accompanying this were their many and varied musical and tuneful styles, and thus their rhythm and *feeling* for the rhythm, all of which would add to the clash of identity and produce something quite unique in its own right.

Of course, some cultures had their own particular way with rhythm and did not alter or evolve, but for example without the Jewish culture, Hollywood simply would not have had a film industry if it were not for such as Irving Berlin and George Gershwin, two giants of the musical idiom and thus the jazz idiom, and whom we still celebrate to this day.

Jazz was essentially a mix of the European standard way of counting and tempo, and the African freewheeling style *and* the Jewish ear for sound and melody and singing. Gershwin is the perfect example of the mix of styles of the Jewish cantor way with song, the classical piano and the feel of the new way that the classical and jazz styles could complement each other: essentially a unique combining of the black (African) and the white (European) ways with rhythm and melody.

Jazz Music

Jazz music is a child of many cultures, but mostly African, and therefore tap is too; it is undeniable that they began to grow up alongside each other from as early as the middle of the nineteenth century. In discussing examples of this mix, senior students of tap identify with American music more readily in their dancing than with other kinds. Why do they appreciate jazz music, jazzy films, jazz singing artists such as Michael Jackson or Aretha Franklin, and jazz-based shows such as *Chicago*? They answer that this music has an energy and is somehow more exciting to dance to when they hear it.

We in England try to emulate and copy this American energized way with our choreography or our music, but in my opinion we only succeed to a certain degree. When comparing original styles such as vaudeville and our 'old time music hall' it is easy to see the difference: one is fast-paced, innovative, free-flowing, glossy and alive, while the other is more ponderous, sedate, quietly witty and falsely grand.

What comes across from this is each country's own character, and whatever we may think of each other, they are both evident and valid. Probably the younger students don't see much of a difference, but in general the older students do prefer, as they would, the more exciting and 'newer' feel of the American culture. The musical, and indeed the genre of musical theatre itself, was, in the early days, called musical comedy; only later in more informed times, when comedy was not the main ingredient in a film with singing (such as in *Jesus Christ Superstar*, *Rent* or *Miss Saigon*) did it adopt the more pertinent title. Nevertheless *musicality was the essential ingredient*, and is so today.

In 1943 the first theatrical showing, and later the film in 1955 of the great musical *Oklahoma*, broke new ground with its decision to replace tap dance as the main dance element with the newer style of

The perfect setting for a tap dance: a ballroom floor, a live band, great lighting and costumes, and an appreciative audience.

jazz and contemporary jazz. In this one show the choreographer Agnes De Mille almost completely abandoned the light-hearted fluffiness of the tap dancer, and instead installed ballet-based and modern dance-based movements as the vehicle for the plot. Drama was needed, and tap didn't really 'do' drama.

De Mille did famously keep a little tap dance, certainly in the film version, when she used the incomparable tap dancer Gene Nelson as a cowboy hoofer for the number 'Kansas City' – a master stroke that successfully married the old dance of tap with the new modern dance. In this way she fulfilled her idea of using tap as a part of the narrative and not just as 'dancer as guest artist', and she was able to do this with her flair for musicality.

After this one production, tap rapidly declined in popularity as the main dance style in film and live theatre. Even in, for example, the film *On The Town*, released in 1949, a great musical comedy of the first order, there is almost no tap dancing, and in the later Astaire features there was little or none in comparison to his earlier films.

In the productions that followed, choreography and its attendant musicality had to reflect the mood and the texture of the songs and of the book itself; it had to aid the narrative. Tap is only ever joyous, but musical theatre has many different feelings to express, and by this time tap had simply run its course, and did not fit with the up-and-coming films with their dramatic content and meaningful storylines.

The most important person taking an audition for a major Broadway or London West End show is the musical director. The actual director and even the producer himself will defer to the MD's choice of performer. Musicality is the key to any show; someone can be slow at learning steps, but if they have the gift of musicality, they will do well at auditions.

When a rhythm tap dancer performs, he or she succeeds *only if it makes musical sense*, or if they possess musicality. This is difficult to define, but might be described as having the ability to convince others that a performance has a rounded quality and a convincing undertone that will impress the audi-

ence. A lot of us probably now possess musicality anyway, but this is because our own mass media constantly affects our every waking moment, feeding us the nuances that go into making it. We are much more musical than at any time, but we don't necessarily know it.

The composer does know it, and it is said that the key to success in a major show that will become a long-running phenomenon is that it possesses at least three 'hook' songs or tunes – so that people will go home singing them and for long after: this is musicality. Such songs are 'Summer Loving', 'Greased Lightning' and 'You're the One That I Want' from the hit show *Grease*, or almost *all* the songs from *Singing in the Rain*!

These shows are appreciated by people of every age. In terms of tap dance, the films that feature it are mostly of the age when Fred Astaire danced in them: this was from the 1930s to the 1950s, and there are none being made at all now. Live shows, on the other hand, are quite regularly revived, and continue to amuse and delight modern audiences. Thus in shows such as *42nd St* and *Crazy For You* we have come to expect expert tap dancing and great songs, enjoyed because of their lasting musicality.

Tap dance has retained the favoured spot in the public's admiration in theatre dance. It is loved unconditionally by the family group, and it cheers and rekindles the spirits whenever it is done properly. One cannot tap *unhappily*: this is a contradiction in terms. In the amateur way, in the dance studio and in a class situation, the same is true. It is, of course, all about the rhythm, and as the wonderful Isolde, mentioned above, said back in the 1930s, rhythm somehow involves *romance*.

I have to believe she was right, because it does indeed connect us all, not least in that old feel-good sense. Rhythm is truly in the very soul of the people and is a life force we all can feel. It's what makes us human. Tap has the unique ability to connect us to this life force because we are making rhythm with our own bodies through our shoes. They connect us to the drum beneath, and the drum is second only to the voice in our human elementals.

CHAPTER 5

BASIC TECHNIQUE

Basically tap technique involves weight transference, balance and the rudiments, which involve certain steps that are the accepted ways to begin.

WEIGHT TRANSFERENCE

Using a definition to describe tap, we might say 'it is only essentially about one thing, and that is changing weight from right foot to left foot, and back again'. It just has to be at super speed, that's all! We might say that *that* is the difficulty, though it becomes easier once the connections between right and left foot are made, or mastered – and they have to be mastered to get any amount of speed. Speed is not essential in order to be a good dancer, and it will come along, rather than be simply there naturally. To gain speed is a choice to be made or not, but in essence it is having clarity that is the mature choice. Practice is the key to doing anything better, and is a requirement in this dance.

What is not so obvious (to the beginner) is how (in the sense of exasperation) do you get to be so controlled at changing weight that you achieve the status of tap dancer? It can seem impossible to the learning eye and ear, and students will often remark that they cannot see what the teacher is doing: it is too fast, they say. At the beginning they are right, it is too hard to see. If you were to look at famous tap dancers on the media and watch film clips of them dancing, it can be both amazing and frightening if you are wanting to learn this thing called tap dancing. For example, look at Gene Nelson, Buster Brown, Dan Dailey, James Cagney, the Dunhills, the Berry brothers and the Condos brothers.

The Condos brothers are a 'must see' if you are keen to explore speed, and took to a whole new level the step previously mentioned called 'wings', a so-called 'flash' step, and an air step, too. These are achieved off the floor, and it's the getting off the floor in the correct way and at incredible speed that gives them their name. I will come to 'wings' in the section below describing advanced techniques, but for now, look at the Condos brothers for their sheer astounding ability with tap shoes. Remember, they had to master a basic technique first, and the speed at which they almost literally fly came along *with incessant practice*. Only in this way can basic technique lead to advanced technique and a performance style (if the latter is what is being sought).

The hobby dancer at an adult age will have to work fairly hard to accomplish these wings, but it is not impossible that they will learn to do them. The child hobby dancer will adapt much more quickly, and could indeed master this step so that a good speed is achieved. It begins with a basic set of rules, one of which is weight transference, and in the case of wings, a very important rule. To achieve this air step the perfect height and the perfect effort has to be learned, and the body constantly 'told' what to do. Dancers use the phrase 'muscle memory', and *only by constant practice* does this occur in the body: only through this constant attention does the body learn exactly how far up and how far out to push the feet. You will see the detail as you progress through this guide.

BALANCE

If we begin on both feet and with the weight perfectly even, we will soon have to decide which foot to move first and which to keep still and in place. This is the classic 'working leg/supporting leg' scenario. To do one thing on one leg we have to do something else with the other leg: we have to use it as a support. Therefore we really cannot be on both legs at once, since to be so we would have no other choice of movement than just jumping up and down on the spot. Hardly tap dancing, but I have seen footage of another one-legged (and indeed one-sided) man do this very thing, but where he is not able to transfer weight at all! You would have to decide for yourself if what he does is actually tap dancing.

Those with perfect balance are the gifted ones, but most of us have to work at it. To have perfect balance will not make us great tap dancers or even great dancers, but it will be a distinct advantage if we have it. While some struggle to know their left from their right, the majority always knows this difference instinctively. Even some dance students check with their finger and thumb on each hand, and look at which one 'spells' L, for left: it will of course be the left hand. But if things are this slow, how do they learn to dance? How do they learn to tap dance, which is a dance of speed and minute shifting of weight? It depends on how much they desire to do it.

To play any instrument it is unquestionably important to learn the basic technique. It is the same with dance, and it must be followed up after every class and at many opportunities – and as the feet are connected to the body, there is no excuse that you have forgotten to bring your instrument with you! The overriding thing about a tap technique is which one to choose, since all styles have a different aspect, a different cultural base, and a different reason to be practised, and some tap dancers will switch techniques if they are not getting what they want from their dancing. In this way I believe the intrinsic style favoured decides the technique, and not the other way round. After, of course, the very basic things such as balance and weight transfer are addressed.

Many of today's younger and more serious tappers would not go near any kind of syllabus or technical framework, for instance, simply because

it will somehow influence their way with the beat or the look. Some dancers are grounded, some are airborne, some are Latin dance based, and some are ballroom based, like Fred Astaire. Some are influenced by the music and some by the dance history. In all these cases the fact remains that the feet must be coordinated and the weight transferred.

Superior balance is required for someone who wants to do lots of off-the-floor things; others like to be *in* the floor and use it to crash and shout with their shoes. Some like to glide and impress with their mastery of their body and muscles to almost hover in their dancing. I know a wonderful teacher in England who almost stands still and moves quite little, *but* the sound coming from his taps defies belief, and he is so close to the floor it is not possible to know what he is doing! His technique *has been developed* and by himself, to accommodate what he is trying to do with his tap dancing; he has adapted to doing what is necessary to achieve his own desired status, and a lot of common technical things have been abandoned in order to focus on what, for him, really matters. However, we almost all need the rudiments.

THE RUDIMENTS

The rudiments consist of the shuffle, the tap step, the pick-up, the paddle, and the connectivity of things.

Set out below are the building blocks of tap, but before moving on to them in detail we should remember that some things are a given, and that both feet have to be coordinated around our balance. Having established that, it is time to move on to those rudimentary things that we have to do to get the sound of the rhythm in our heads out on to the floor via our taps.

So exactly *what* do we need to learn so that we are tap dancing? We cannot just stamp around, and so we must use those tried and tested ways with the feet and tap shoes that have been around for decades. Here I refer to steps such as the shuffle, the tap step and the pick-up. All of these, and many more, are the basic elements or, as I am calling

Another example of a toe tap that is older and more basic, though still with the option of toning via the screw fixings.

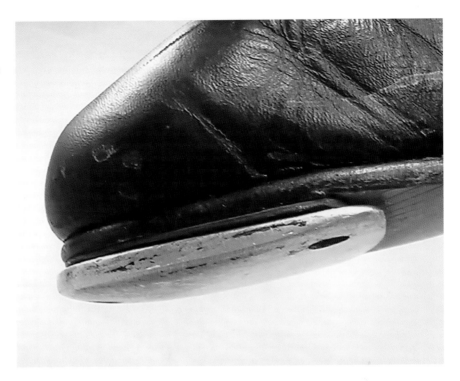

NOTE

'Tapping' is when the tap hits the floor and lifts off again, achieved by flexing the ankle; 'beating' is the sound made when the toe is held down on to the floor after hitting. One is carrying a light sound, and the other a heavier, more sustained sound.

Brushing describes itself in that the toe tap hits in a forward or backward motion, lifting the shoe off the floor in a sweeping (brushing) motion. If done forwards it is known as a forward brush, but done backwards it is called a pick-up or a pull-back. As the heel also has a tap on it, a forward heel brush is also possible.

Stepping on to the ball of the brushing foot and using the toe tap to brush, we have the sound of a 'tap step', and a 'pick-up step' if we do this action backwards. Because a step bears the weight and stays down, it is obviously a beat.

Brush Toe. 1. Lift the heel and prepare to 'kick' the foot forwards...

2. ...strike the toe tap forwards and long...

3. ...point the foot as it goes through the action.

them, the *rudiments*, which are the accepted ways to begin. So we need to know what they are in isolation: how do we do a shuffle, a tap step and a pick-up? How do we utilize the building blocks?

Knowing where the taps are on our shoes will help: the toe tap is just under the front part of the sole and therefore under the toes themselves, and the heel tap covers the whole heel behind. Just behind the toe tap is the part of the shoe that I consider to be very important, and that is the ball of the foot – important because that is where the weight transfers in the main. The whole foot will incorporate both heel and toe sounds if you land on it fully, as in stamping, and that is also a legitimate way of changing weight.

With the toe tap we can produce a huge amount of sound by tapping, beating, brushing and landing with weight.

In general terms the toe is used in a lighter fashion or for lighter sounds, and the heel for an emphatic sound, rather like a snare drum and a base drum. A variety of sounds are needed, and the shoes can produce a remarkable array of them on educated

Brush Heel. 1. Lift the heel and prepare to 'kick' the foot forwards...

2. ...strike the point of the heel forwards...

3. ...point the foot as it goes through the action.

The Shuffle. 1. Prepare to lift the toe tap from the floor...

2. ...lift the toe by bending the knee backwards and flexing the ankle...

3. ...brush the toe tap forwards and strike the floor, again flexing the ankle...

4. ...strike the toe tap backwards on the return...

5. ...again flex the ankle up and back to gain a clear sound.

feet. Just the act of stepping on to the ball of the foot is the basic weight change, and this will always be a heavy or an emphatic sound.

The Shuffle

The shuffle is a brushing movement, and with the toe tap only. Stand with the weight on one foot and with that leg slightly bent (not ramrod straight), and with the weight tilted forwards. Lift the other foot from the floor and gain a balanced state. Pull the foot upwards and backwards from the floor, and brush the toe tap forwards and up and then back and up with the rhythm a1, a2, a3, and so on. This is an accented sound, and the shuffle must always have this accented sound. If it is a brush forwards and back without this accent, it is just a brush forwards and a brush back; the shuffle depends on this rhythm aspect.

Also it is usually taught with the emphasis more on the backward motion, but better than that is the addition of an up-and-down action of the knee at the same time. This lifting of the knee will add a

sharpness to the brushing action, and because it involves both ankle and knee the dancer will build to good and neat dexterity.

The Shuffle Step

The shuffle step is the same as the above but with the addition of the foot coming down on to the floor afterwards. Doing as the words say, it is now a shuffle and then a step with the same foot, and usually on the ball of foot. This counts as follows: a1 2, a3 4, and so on.

The Shuffle Step Heel

The shuffle step heel is the same as the above, but with the addition of the heel. This is done on the same foot and counts thus: a1 a2; a3 4; a5 6; a7 a8, and so on. If we do alternate feet, first one then the other, we are already building on our basic technique by adding the change of weight. Hopefully it becomes evident that we are simply adding and expanding the action to build new 'steps' or figures.

The Shuffle Step.   1. Prepare to lift the toe tap from the floor...

2. ...strike the toe tap forwards and up, flexing the ankle...

3. ...strike the toe tap backwards and up on the return, flexing the ankle for a clear sound...

4. ...put the ball of the foot down with a positive action...

5. ...change the weight fully into the step, but still on the ball of foot.

The Shuffle Step Heel.   1. Prepare to lift the toe tap...

2. ...flexing the ankle ...

3. ...strike the toe tap forwards and up, flexing the ankle...

4. ...strike the toe tap backwards and up on the return, flexing the ankle for a clear sound...

5. ...step down on to the ball of foot with a positive action and changing weight into it...

6. ...add a heel beat with a positive action to complete the change of weight.

The Tap Step (Flaps)

Standing on one foot and establishing your balance, lift the other foot off the floor and pull it slightly back ready to strike the floor forwards and with the toe tap. Landing or changing weight into this foot will give us our *tap step*. Do not put the heel down. This is a walking or travelling step and should be practised as a means of gaining momentum and moving from the spot. It self-describes, and is one of the essentials of tap dancing.

In various syllabuses this is called a 'tap step' because that is what is happening: a tap followed by a change of weight, the step. However, a better way for the tap step is the shorter, sharper version, described as a 'flap'. The American tap dancer probably does not know the phrase 'tap step', but he will know the word 'flap' to describe the action. This is because traditionally it is done with a downward and tight feel, with the toe landing very sharply and the knee lifting upwards and not backwards for the next one on the other leg. It almost looks like a

Tap Step. **1. Stand on one leg and prepare to lift the other…**

2. …lifting the leg, flex the ankle and start to push the foot forwards…

3. …strike the toe tap down and forwards in a sharp action…

4. ...a properly flexed ankle will add to the emphasis...

5. ...step with a positive beat on the ball of the foot and change the weight into it with either a straight or a bent knee.

marching action, and with a strutting feeling on the balls of the feet – and of course we have another form of change of weight.

A higher knee lift to the front is the main difference, and the dancer taught by an established syllabus method will often find this awkward to master. This is an essential figure, but the difference in the action will confuse some dancers for a while because it is almost a reverse of what is asked for in some alternative instructions; it lifts the leg in front and not behind, it lands with an almost straightened leg and not sinking down into the floor with the knee bending, and it is short and sharp and not a long step. The foot is flexed at the ankle to give a shorter and sharper action into the floor. It is less of a brush and can thus be utilized for great speed; a normal tap step will be slower by comparison.

The Pick-Up Step

Standing on the supporting leg and gaining your balance, lift the toe tap of the working leg off the floor, in a hinge-like fashion leaving the heel down. At this point the ankle is flexed, which lifts the toe off the floor. Striking the toe tap backwards and upwards give us a single sound as the toe tap 'picks up' from the floor. Transferring weight on to this foot behind, and on the ball, gives us the step, and we have now the whole pick-up step. If we stay on the balls of both feet we can now do the other foot, but we must have a momentum backwards and stay in balance whilst we do this.

If we continue to advance backwards by lowering the heel we can do so, providing the heel is silent. Some styles allow the heel to go down, and this is a rolling of the foot through the ball to the heel and gives a more natural walking action as it progresses – rather as we would if actually walking backwards. This is particularly useful when teaching adults because it is a more natural progressing action and resembles walking.

Pick-Up Step.   1. With the foot flat on the floor prepare to lift the toe tap...

2. ...lift the toe but keep the heel down...

3. ...strike the toe tap firmly down on the pulling back action...

4. ...continue to strike backwards, and lift and flex the ankle to accentuate the sound, ready to land the foot behind on the ball...

5. ...land on the ball of the foot and change the weight into the foot.

The Paddle

The paddle is rather like the shuffle with two sounds and coming off the floor in execution. It is, however, much faster and lower than the shuffle, so multiple sounds can become very quick. To do this, stand on one leg and lift the heel of the other, bring the foot forwards and dig the heel into the floor where the leg extends and do not lift from the floor. Immediately bring the foot back and catch the toe tap on the way to produce two sounds. In the shuffle I would advocate using the ankle mainly, but in the paddle it should be the mainly the knee, since to over-use the ankle here will produce a weaker sound.

The Paddle Step

As with the shuffle, just adding the step will give us three sounds; when this is done one foot followed by the other we can gain tremendous speed with this step because it is so low to the floor and we are poised on the balls of the feet.

The Paddle. 1. Lift the weight from the heel by bending the foot...

2. ...strike the rear edge of the heel into the floor with a 'digging' action...

3. ...bend the knee backwards and up, at the same time striking the floor with the toe tap as in the shuffle action.

The Paddle Step. 1. Lift the weight from the heel by bending the foot…

2. …strike the rear edge of the heel into the floor with a 'digging' action…

3. ...bend the knee backwards and up, and strike the toe tap...

4. ...put the weight fully into the ball of foot.

The Paddle Step Heel

The original name for this exciting step is a 'paddle and roll', and not, as some say currently, a 'para-diddle'. That is a drummer's term and is misnamed because it *sounds* like the paradiddle of the drummer. It is, however, almost as fast as a drummer's hands can go and with relatively little effort, because we are even lower to the floor than when using the paddle step. The paddle step is on the balls of the feet, but the paddle step heel stays in the plié and can progress into great speed.

CONNECTIVITY

The above few paragraphs hopefully show that this adding of things, or 'connectivity', is a very good and easily understandable way to learn to tap. I use an 'addition' system as a means of instilling some kind of format in the learner's brain; otherwise I feel the steps and taps can all become quite jumbled in the head. There has to be a vocabulary, and even rhythm tappers who may say they are entirely improvisa-tional have already had to go through the basics. If one does a shuffle and then a step on the ball of foot and then a heel beat, this then becomes one thing and not three separate things. Thus it is pronounced a *shuffle step heel*, which would seem to make perfect sense. Adding a hop and a stamp we can say it is a *shuffle hop step heel stamp*, and hope the learner would see what is being danced. (*See* my book *Teach Yourself Tap Dancing* Hodder, 2007.)

It's an ABC sort of method, and for the amateur dancer in the dance studio it is the line of most sense; it also sounds right phonetically, with a matching syllable sound.

This connectivity of the A and the B and the C looks reasonable to the learner because it 'says' what it means by stringing together the names of the rudiments we all must learn first. Therefore, a list of the basic foot movements (building blocks) is required for this rudimental way of connect-ing. Below can be seen the basic sounds and then examples of the addition of other basic sounds to produce rudimentary figures such as the shuffle and

The Paddle Step Heel.   1. Lift the heel...

2. ...strike the back of the heel into the floor...

3. ...knee backwards and up to strike the toe tap...

4. ...change the weight into the ball of foot...

5. ...add a heel beat with a positive action and complete the change of weight.

the paddle, which will then be added to produce more basic sets of sounds, and so on.

A LIST OF TERMINOLOGY

step: On the ball of the foot with a natural transfer of weight.

stamp: On the whole foot, with a change of weight.

brush: With toe tap or heel tap.

scuff: Whole foot brushed forwards with intention.

spring: Jumping from one foot to the other in a 'dropping' action.

stomp: On the whole foot, without a change of weight.

tap: Strike the toe tap either in place or forwards without change of weight.

hop: Spring from one foot *to the same foot* (*no weight change*). (*See* photograph.)

pick up: One sound made backwards with a brush of the toe tap.

heel beat: Heel down hard and staying down.

heel tap: Heel down hard and lifting again.

heel brush: Forwards.

heel 'dig': When the back of the heel digs into the floor.

toe tip: The tip of the toe is hit and lifted off the floor.

ball change: Ball of the foot R, change weight to L with a step.

ball heel, or step heel: Adding two of the above.

heel ball: Adding two of the above and using both feet in a transfer.

shuffle: A brush forward and backward with the toe tap to the rhythm 'a1'.

paddle: A heel dig in front followed by a brush back with the toe tap.

tap step: Adding a tap and a step together.

pick-up step: Adding two of the above things together.

double pick-up: An advanced step, using both feet almost at once and landing on the balls of both feet. In the air it is: 'pick-up pick-up, step, step' (R L, R L).

The list is not quite exhaustive, but what is certainly not exhaustive is the combining of these things to achieve many thousands of longer things. It is this notion of combining that leads to tap dancing, and I again stress it is simply a way of constructing things (vocabulary) in a rhythmic fashion so that it becomes a rhythmic language.

This is so easy to grasp as a concept it is often surprising that people sometimes find it difficult to learn tap dance. Rather like speaking, we all want to express ourselves, and we feel we can *if we have the words*. With tap we can *if we have the rudiments*. If the rudiments are learned and practised one at a time and then joined, we will arrive at a new thing, a dance piece. Rather as in a train, say, we build each carriage, with its hundreds of tiny elements, and we then join all these carriages together. Only then is it the single entity that we can call a train.

So now let us build a simple 'train'. Below are the basic elements needed to build, in tap dance terms, a *time step*. But before that we need to know the answer to the question: 'What is a time step?'

THE TIME STEP

In the 'Tap History Culture' section at the beginning of this book I mentioned King Rastus Brown as being

The stamp: Land the full foot down as hard as is required, with a bent knee and a change of weight. This can be to the front or to the side, or crossed over.

The stomp: Land the full foot down as hard as is required, with a bent knee and NO change of weight. This can be to the front or to the side, or crossed over.

Heel dig: An action into the floor with the back of the heel, without weight.

Toe tip: Strike the toe down into the floor without weight, in any position. Using toe stands the weight is transferred one after the other quickly.

the inventor of the time step. In the days of travelling shows such as the medicine and minstrel shows in the nineteenth century, all dance acts that tapped had a 'timing step' of their own to demonstrate to the band or orchestra in the towns and cities they visited just how fast to play their music. This was vital, because a lot of variation in this respect could meet with the audience's disapproval, and also the management's if they were heard to be 'out of time'.

The band leader would ask for the timing, and the act would have a special dance routine to show this. There could be several different timings if there were musical changes, and thus the timing step would be demonstrated at these speeds. In due course this timing step idea became a standardized require-ment, and most of the acts would use the same one, albeit with variations. The time step described below is generally recognized globally (among those countries who do tap, obviously).

This evolved step is a product of years of dancing and of many dancers. What I describe below is just one example, but any combination step, if it does the following four things, can be called a time step. The four principles are as follows:

1. It REPEATS from right side to left side and again to the right side, using the same combining idea of the basics listed above, on each side.
2. It uses the SAME NUMBER OF COUNTS on both sides: four counts on the right, four counts on the left, four on the right again (*see* note below).
3. Using this 'three sides' format we leave the fourth bar of four free for the hotly anticipated BREAK.
4. IT KEEPS YOU IN TIME over the usual measure of FOUR bars for the traditional jazz phrasing.

NOTE: I use the longer version eight counts phrasing because that has always been evident in the music. And in fact using eight counts in the 'dancer's' bar is both easier and more practical to give the body more freedom to use the body. A musician uses the standard four counts to his bar; the dancer uses the traditional eight counts to his bar. This is entirely an

American invention, and it is because jazz dance is an American invention; hence the time-honoured expression that even non-dancers know: 'a 5 6 7 8!' when a dance is beginning. It is the count into the routine, the 'ready, steady, go' of the typical jazz dancer.

Back to the historical time step and the *four* counts each side. You will note that the first count written is an eight because it is part of this wholly traditional aspect, and for the purposes of this book we will stick to the traditional way. Because so much of dance is steeped in tradition we are hard pressed to change it, even if we could; we may as well try to rename Easter. Here in this book we are concerned with things how they are *now*. The time step described below is in a four round of counts, but everywhere the reader will find it, it will be counted as two eights. Four fours are two eights, and I can find no answer as to quite why it was ever estab-lished in this way. So let us just stick to tradition.

The Single Time Step

The time step is in *four* counts because it is linked traditionally with music phrasing in the early days of jazz and the introduction of the revolutionary 4/4. We need to show three things to help in the expla-nation:

- what count we are doing
- what we are doing physically
- on which foot we are doing these

To do this *at the same time* I will write as follows:

8	and	1	2	and	3	and
shuffle		hop	spring	tap step		step
R		L	R	L		R

4	and	5	6	and	7	and
shuffle		hop	spring	tap step		step
L		R	L	R		L

Duly noting the count of 8 at the beginning, we can move on to say that the *single* part of the time step on the right foot falls on the '2' (it has a single sound), and we see that each side will take *four counts* and be repeated three times (three bars) until the 'break' comes along on the fourth bar; as mentioned, three bars of the same thing is the time step, and the fourth bar is the 'break'. (*See below* for the 'break'.)

Concentrating on the first side only with the weight on the left foot, we are ready to shuffle on our right foot in the above rhythm. Notice the underlines on three steps: this is done to illustrate the emphasis on those feet when the weight changes into them. By doing this we achieve a more rhythmic sound, and one that we can say has a definite swing to it.

Also on the last change, the '3and', we have the first *syncopation*. To reiterate from above, by stressing the 'and' we achieve the opposite of the norm (which is to stress the number itself) – stressing the 'and' gives us a different percussive feel, and it is one which tap dancers the world over strive for. I feel it important to go over again what is meant by syncopating in rhythm, because in no way can this be understated! Therefore, in somewhat simple terms, forgive this reiteration:

> ** Syncopation is when the stress falls on the part of the count that is not normally stressed (the off beat) and rhythm is rarely possible without syncopation. It is literally the thing that defines rhythm, and to not have this syncopation is to have only tempo.*

Back to the time step, and obviously if there is a single time step there is probably a double and a triple and a quadruple. In addition, each one can then be prefaced by saying a shuffle (time step) or a stamp (time step) or a paddle (time step) or a stamp pick-up (time step). The example above begins with the shuffle, therefore it is denoting the kind of time step. If we do a stamp it changes to that, and so on. In this way quite a large amount of variation is attainable.

Also again: each of these can have more extra things! So we could have a 'shuffle, pick-up change' time step or a 'stamp, double pick-up' time step or a 'shuffle, wing' time step.

The list of time steps then is quite impressive, and it proves my theory that if you *add* elements together in an ever more creative way, the result will be a complexity of great proportions. And all on just two feet!

The Double Time Step

Looking below at the counting, it is easy to see where the difference is between the 1 and 2. Count this as follows, as 'and 2':

8	and	1	and	2	and	3	and
shuffle	hop		tap	spring	tap	step	step
R	L			R		L	R

4	and	5	and	6	and	7	and
shuffle	hop		tap	spring	tap	step	step
L	R			L		R	L

At this juncture I am hoping sincerely that the reader is not confused! It is only the addition of one sound that gives it the title of 'double'. And the idea of that one sound extra is repeated again in the triple, as follows.

The Triple Time Step

Look for the addition between these two numbers, and count this as 'and a 2', with the 'and a 2' the triple sound:

8	and	1	and	a	2	and	3	and
shuffle	hop		sh		spring	tap	step	step
R	L				R		L	R

4	and	5	and	a	6	and	7	and
shuffle	hop		sh		spring	tap	step	step
L	R				L		R	L

To go further into a time step that has four sounds, and could be called a quadruple (though this is entirely my own invention), just add the heel beat after the shuffle spring. Count this quadruple time step then as: 'and and a 2' for the four sounds, where previously there have been one and two and three.

8	and	1	and	and	a	2	an	3	and
shuffle	<u>hop</u>	sh	spring	<u>heel</u>		tap	step		step
R	L		R				L		R

4	and	5	and	and	a	6	and	7	and
shuffle	<u>hop</u>	sh	spring	<u>heel</u>		tap	step		step
L	R		L				R		L

The Break

For the purposes of clarity the 'break' as described here will be the same for all four of the above time steps: single, double, triple and quadruple. However, the break actually is the one free thing in most time steps that can add an interest; it can be the final individual expression after the time step has been set up. To change the break is ideally the thing to go for: to do something out of the norm and original. In tap dancing this is what the dancer constantly aims to do, to bring out of the floor something that nobody has seen or that nobody else has thought of doing. As the song by Crosby and Armstrong says: 'Now you has jazz!'

All right, we have managed to do two of the three sides of any one of the time steps above, and the break as described here is the traditional one because the time steps above are traditional. Bearing in mind that even these are subject to differences according to the many syllabuses published, it is safer to say this is the standard break and go ahead and describe it.

After landing on the spring on the count of 2 on the third side (having done the R side and then the L side and now the R side again) we complete the rest of the whole figure by switching into the following rhythm: 2 and 3 and 4 and 5 and 6 and 7. This is an even sound and is achieved by doing three shuffle steps, after this spring, on the L and the R and L again. It all ends with a step or a stamp on the last foot (the R) on the count of 7. The last two sounds are a ball change in rhythm.

Count and say this break as follows:

and	3	and	4	and	5	and	6	and	7
shuffle	step		shuffle	step		shuffle	step		step
	L			R			L		R

Count the whole time step and break *on the third side* as follows, in the single time step:

8 and 1 2 and 3 and 4 and 5 and 6 and 7

Note the gap between the 1 and the 2 to denote it is a single time step, with one sound on the 2 count.

TIMING AND COUNTING

The whole point of a time step is to keep the dancer in time to the music, and although this is obvious to most people, often the dancer has to be constantly reminded. We are but human after all, and recorded music is entirely different; a machine will not adjust its speed to suit the dancer, so he or she has to do any adjusting, and constantly. To 'have an ear' in dance is either a gift or one to be found through practice; either way we all must adhere to the beat and what it does for us.

Timing is as the tuneful note that accompanies the word on the music sheet. If the word and the note are not in tune or 'in sync', the note will be known as flat and as such will be of no real value. A song has a mixture of disciplines and tap has similar disciplines, all having to be melded into the one thing. They both have a basic set of rules, rely on proper practice, build from the basics to the elementary and then to the more advanced stages, have to go through a technique regimen, and have an end product.

We can do the steps, but if they are not in time we will be dancing wrongly and the observer will be unimpressed. If we do not have this 'ear' for timing – and many dancers don't – we are not dancing completely. The enjoyment in tap dancing is gained through this ear, and of course the visual aspect is also fairly vital – otherwise why would anyone learn it? It is such a satisfying thing to do, and it has to do with the music. The time step is not a beginner's step, but it does use the elementals and those basic foot movements from our glossary.

I always begin a class by transferring weight, by

NOTE

The simplest explanation of this difference between tempo and rhythm is that in practically any song the sung line or melody line will be the rhythm, and the regularity and speed of the supporting percussion section will set and hold the tempo. All of the instruments in a band are playing their own syncopated sound, and all are layered on top of the agreed tempo set by themselves.

stepping from one foot to another in time to the music track that's playing. I use the *tempo* of the music first in the warm-up period, and I only do this stepping or changing weight motion as a beginning. I state where the balance should be, and that it is forward or tilted forward to gain maximum impact and immediate transfer from each foot. Tap begins with just *one* sound and that is stepping, as in walking. Next, I do this stepping or weight transfer from foot to foot *in rhythm* insisting people are *on time* with the tempo. It is very important to make sure everyone knows the difference between tempo and rhythm, because not everyone does (*see* Note box)!

Next in teaching a class I introduce the 'swing note' (*see* above: Rhythm and Music); this is the base of most of tap dance because it is the base of so much of jazz music, the music of tap. To see this sound and what this looks like in print let us have an example:

The first line set out below is the count of a bar of music using eight counts per bar. As mentioned above, dance is usually expressed in counts of eight to a bar and not four to a bar. This is a typical American jazz dance idiom and marks the tempo. Tempo is usually measured in *quarter notes*, and this needs explaining, too.

Purely in dancer terms, we can split the counts into *seven separate note values*. They are:

Whole note (one count is held for the duration of four beats, or four quarter notes before saying the second count)

Half note (one count is held for the duration of two quarter notes)

Quarter note (we measure tempo of the bar in these notes. All counts in the following sections are expressed in quarter notes)

Eighth notes (twice as fast as quarter notes and using the 'and' notation, as in: and 1 and 2 and 3 etc)

Twelfth notes (again faster, but not twice as fast, and using the 'and a' notation, as in: and a 1, and a 2, and a 3 etc)

Sixteenth note (twice as fast as the eighth note and using the 'and and a' notation, as in: and and a 1, and and a 2, and and a 3 etc). Of course twice as fast as the eighth note is equal to four times the speed of the quarter note, so that in just one count there are four very quick sounds. Remember we are splitting each count fractionally.

Accented eighth note (this is our old friend the swing note and uses the 'a' notation, as in a1, a2, a3 etc)

All jazz 4/4 rhythms can be broken down into the above parts, and it is a good but also fairly laborious task for the dancer to have to count them. Still, it sharpens the brain and the feet!

All bars in the 4/4 construction are measured in quarter notes, as stated above – indeed the very expression 4/4 means that the lower figure is the value and the upper figure is the quantity of them in the bar; thus in a 4/4 there are four quarter notes signified. If the music is in a waltz construction of 3/4, there are three quarter notes in the bar.

Quarter notes:

1 2 3 4 5 6 7 8; 1 2 3 4 5 6 7 8; 1

The second line below is how to count the swing note, and should be said as it is seen – but note the gaps between each number, which will give us the swing element.

a1 a2 a3 a4 a5 a6 a7 a8; a1 a2 a3 a4 a5 a6 a7 a8; a1

As mentioned above, it is called a swing note because it allies itself to the way we walk and exist in this swinging fashion, by the use of the arms and the legs occurring in a natural gait. It also occurs when we step from heel to toe in each and every step: heel down first then the ball, giving two soft sounds but nevertheless two sounds in our natural footfall. When we walk down stairs we naturally reverse this to toe, then heel.

Also of note is that the heart itself has this double sound, and we can hear it saying to us: a1, a2, a3, a4 etc. No wonder we like to tap dance, or at least appreciate it if we see it done well: it belongs to the body!

It is no surprise that the rudimental steps above are in this swing fashion. We have at this point now brought together the theory and the practical execution of tap dance, because the practical action in the swing note of the *shuffle* is in an 'a1 a2 a3 a4' operation; the *tap step* says 'a1 a2 a3 a4', and the *pick-up step* says the same. Each has two sounds with the second being the heavier one, and this *accenting* is essential to understand.

The majority of tap dancing exists in this rhythm, and it is truly the signature sound of the genre: the body has a natural affinity to this swinging way of moving. Quite why that is so is a matter for the anthropologist, but it is hard to deny that hearing a swing sound will get our feet moving. A perfect combination to illustrate this swing thing is the tap dancer's signature step, the shim sham.

THE SHIM SHAM

Another time step, the shim sham, deserves a mention here because without it a book on tap dance would be considered incomplete. Invented by a Native American called Leonard Reed in the late 1920s, it is a combination step used by tap dancers in all corners of the world, and still retains its position as the quintessential feature of choice of the serious tapper. It has the standard eight counts to a bar of the dancer, and not four counts to the bar of the musician. It lasts for thirty-two counts (four dancer's bars of eight counts per bar).

As with the other standardized time step above, it is a collection of basic rudiments such as shuffle, step, toe, hop and heel. The difference in them is quite stark in that one is obviously a musician's invention, while the other is a tap (jazz) dancer's invention designed to actually dance to. Also, the time step is so standardized by now that it has become almost a fossil, but it does serve a purpose in that it creates a sort of bench mark for all the learners going into the world of tap dance, from child to adult.

The shim sham is not referred to as a time step, but it is one because it exhibits exactly the same attributes of a time step and therefore can be called one. (*See* above on the basic principles.)

NOTE

The differences in the American way and the sometimes called 'English' way of teaching tap exist in the way with the words: the American way uses many phrases such as the 'shim sham' or the 'Suzie-Q', so their method of teaching can be very different and more relaxed and colloquial. The English way depends more on the naming of the individual steps in the shim sham, such as 'shuffle step, shuffle step, shuffle ball-change, shuffle step', which actually describes what is happening.

There are *four* parts to this iconic mix of tap rudiments: the shim sham, the cross-over, the Tack Annie and the Falling Off a Log.

Briefly, the *timing* goes like this for the first part (shim sham):

8 and 1, 2 and 3, 4 and 5 and 6 and 7   ON THE R FOOT

8 and 1, 2 and 3, 4 and 5 and 6 and 7   ON THE L FOOT

8 and 1, 2 and 3, 4 and 5 and 6 and 7   ON THE R FOOT All of this is the time step itself, and following is the break:

8   1   2   3 and   and 5   6   7

Note the syncopation with the two 'and and' together, which gives us the accenting of the off beat of the '3 and'.

Now we can add the names (in abbreviated form) of the steps to see what we are actually doing:

On the right foot:

8	and	1	2	and	3	4	and	5	and	6	and	7
shfl		stp	shfl		stp	shfl		ball	ch	shfl		stp
R			L			R		R	L	R		

Repeat on the left foot. Repeat on the right foot again. Then add the break as follows:

8	1	2	3	and	a	5	6	7
stp	heel	toe tip	heel	stp	heel	stp	stp	stp
R	R	L	R	L	L	R	L	R

Shim Sham Break. 1. Using the R foot, step into the ball of the foot and follow this with a strong heel beat...

2. ...use a toe tap of the L foot to strike behind the R...

3. ...heel-step R L, changing weight into the L ball of the foot...

4. ...heel-step L R, changing weight into the R ball of the foot, crossing behind...

5. ...step into the L ball of the foot...

6. ...bring the feet together R into the L.

The toe sound is with the tip of the toe tap, and should be seen as being crossed behind the R foot, which makes the heel sound. The heel step, heel step travels from the spot to the left and finishes with the feet together. Refer to the pictures again to see this progression.

Added to the first three 8s is the 'shimmy', which is variously described, but here as 'the rapid shaking of the shoulders back and forth'. This is done at the same time if the dancer is sufficiently coordinated! This will require quite a bit of concentration, but it is worth the effort, and when done correctly the tap dancer will be connecting historically with all those proper tap dancers who have gone before. It is the tap dancer's signature step.

The second part (the cross-over) is the easiest, and is as follows (all steps are on the ball of the foot):

8	1	2	3	4	5	and	a 7
stamp	stp	stamp	stp	stp	heel-ball		heel-ball
R	L	R	L	R	R	L	L R

The 'stp heel-ball heel-ball' is the cross-over travelling to the R, with the L going over the R. Because there is a '5 and' this gives us the syncopated stress using this off beat feature. The heel-ball is the heel of one foot, and the ball of the other foot.

This is done on the right, then left, then the right, and the break is the cross-over itself, as follows:

8	1	and	and	3	4	5	and	and	7
stp	heel-ball		heel-ball		stp	heel-ball		heel-ball	
L	L-R		R-L		R	R-L		L-R	

Cross-Over. 1. Using the R foot, step into the ball of the foot on count '8', stepping back on to the L on count '1'. Repeat this on counts '2 3'...

2. ...do a ball beat with the R followed by a heel of the R, then cross-over with the L ball of the foot on counts '4 5 and'...

3. ...using the L heel on the count 'and', followed by the...

4. ...ball beat on the R on count '7'

The third part – the Tack Annie – is another of those names passed down from year to year and dancer to dancer for reasons lost to all, but which serves a purpose. It has the following timing:

and	8	and	1	2	and	3	4	and	5	6	and	7
stmp	stmp	pkup	stp	stmp	pkup	stp	stmp	pkup	stp	stmp	pkup	stp
L	R		L		L	R		R	L		L	R

Repeat all of this *on the same foot* (which makes this a unique time step because it does not change sides; still, it does keep us in time, it lasts for eight counts, and has a break!).

The break is the same break from the first part of the shim sham above.

The fourth part (Falling Off a Log) is the essence of the big finish and can be relied upon to give all who are hearing or doing it a good feeling of achievement.

The timing is as follows:

8	1	and	2	and	3	4	5	and	6	and	7
stmp	stp	shuffle		ball	chnge	stmp	stp	shuffle		ball	chnge
R	L	R		R	L	R	L	R		R	L

Repeat this on the same foot, R.

Now the break from the earlier shim sham comes in again on the R to end with the weight on the right foot, ready to do the whole of the 'Log' on the other side, the left. At this point the thirty-two-bar chorus is completed.

There are many alternatives to the finish of the 'Log' part, and this is open to the interpretation of the dancer or dancers.

A BASIC AMALGAMATION

A tap dance routine is what a great many people want from a class, and also what a professional student wants too, to prepare for an audition. The professional dancer also likes to feel they have actually *danced* in a class, and it is the final flourish to the session. Tap is so universal it is almost impossible to leave a class down-hearted or sad, unless the teacher is not doing a good job – in which case another teacher needs to be found. With a public class situation people tend to go as much for the teacher as the subject. Style is an attractive package, and teachers have their own particular ways and means. This is quite normal, and has been the hallmark of the drop-in class for years.

We need to establish boundaries for our amalgamation, such as how fast the music will be, and how much it has in its character to help with the steps.

As discussed above, the phrasing and the dynamics are important, and even at this level they are needed and can be used. I will leave the choice of music to the reader, but I now suggest for you to try at home with the parameters below.

The Music

I will suggest a 'big band' sound here because it is usually a solid sound with a good beat and lots of instrumentation. With this aspect the dancer can home in on a particular instrument and use that for the rhythm choice – *or* he or she can just use the pace or the tempo and follow that. It is important to like the music, too, because that will help enormously to get the feet to respond.

The Tempo

Choose a track that interests you, and not just because it has the right speed. Speed comes along with practice, and anyway it isn't the major factor in a tap dance routine: that factor is clarity or precision and will take time to master. I would suggest even Van Gogh didn't achieve anything at the first try. Rather, the process is the joy, just as much as the finished product.

The Surface

If ever there was a problem specifically attached to tap dancing it is the *floor*. If the reader lives in a loft conversion, or has a wooden floor that can take a pair of tap shoes pounding on it, or lives on the ground floor of flats or apartments with a wooden floor, or has his or her own private studio at home (!), there will be no problem. If, as for most of us, these are not available, simply buy a board measuring in total say 3m by 2m and about 15mm thick (of course in pieces will make this easier to handle). All is dependent on the reader's own circumstances.

Failing any of these, why not try the yard, or the cellar, or the garden decking? In truth, the floor situation could be the factor that stops a lot of people tap dancing, so it is a consideration of no small proportions. The best place is usually the kitchen floor (but not the kitchen worktop, as someone once told me they used!).

The Shoes

Shoes are discussed at length later, but for now, assuming the shoes are of leather and quite rigid, and certainly not trainers, we are ready to contemplate a beginner's or a basic routine to practise. I will use the sort of language and abbreviations that I used above, and hope that this will give you help and inspiration. It really is a question of understanding the basics and repeating them, as with any other technique: what we need is the will to practise and repeat.

We will use the following principles: weight transference, shuffles, hops, ball-changes, stamps and tap-steps. And eight bars of eight counts each. Begin with the weight on the L, and do as follows:

A: tp-stp R, tp-stp L, shuffle bll-ch stp R, hop-step, step R L R;
count: a1   a2   a3   a4   5   a7   8;

B: stamp step L R, stamp step L R, ball L heel-ball LR, heel-ball RL;
(this bar is the Cross Over from the Shim Sham on the L, but on count 1).
Count: 1   2   3   4   5   6 and   and 8;
A and B. Repeat

C: bll-ch step (R L R to right side, dragging L closing to R)
Repeat on the other foot

Count: (miss 1)   a2   3   (miss 4)   a5   6   (miss 7 and 8)

Repeat the whole of C again.

D: Single time step and break on count 8 on R from above technique.
Count: 8 and 1, 2 and 3 and
4 and 5, 6 and 7 and
8 and 1, 2 and 3 and 4 and 5 and 6 and 7

If the reader can do this amalgamation and the shim sham before, after some practice and perseverance, he or she should consider they have achieved very much if they are relatively inexperienced. Although this is a basic combination, it is made up of elements that first have to be learned and practised. This aspect is vital, and will take time – but that is the point, of course. Practice is nothing less than essential with tap dance because it is an instrument, after all, and needs care and attention.

At this point we should consider how to 'see' rhythm. Seeing sound in figures and in diagram form is a good way to learn how to count. Most of the time almost all of us can repeat a given simple rhythm. For instance, we can easily repeat the rhythm of the tune 'Happy Birthday', or a piece from a favourite song. This can be from a show or from a popular era the reader is familiar with.

We all know a great many tunes, and in our heads there are probably thousands of these little rhythmic pieces. We don't necessarily have to be able to count

them, but it helps to at least know *how* to count. Of course, the student will only really want to imitate the teacher, and this is fine. When the student goes home to practise, however, the teacher may not go with them, and so they must retain the rhythm from the class in their head in order to practise. It is not possible to stress enough the importance of practice in tap dance.

'The rhythm clock' is my own idea which I hope gives a helpful visual dimension to understanding rhythm.

THE RHYTHM CLOCK

As with an actual clock, the idea, takes the shape of a circle with figures. However, with the rhythm clock there are eight figures and not twelve. This is the standard eight count for the jazz base for dancers, and it is possible to write the rhythm in a circle and not along a line. I have perfected this idea, and proved it can work in all circumstances;

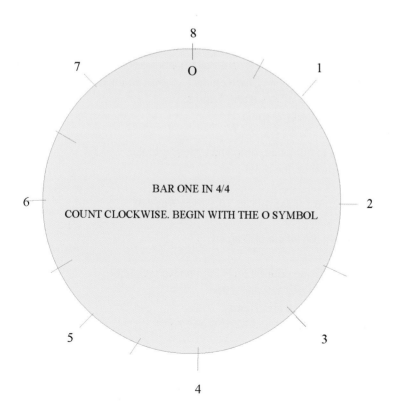

BAR ONE IN 4/4

COUNT CLOCKWISE. BEGIN WITH THE O SYMBOL

Rhythm clock: reading clockwise, start at the 0 and say only what is marked on the clock. In this case count '8 and 1, 2 and 3, 4 and 5 and 6 and 7'. This is the rhythm of the first part of the shim sham.

below is a typical example of a rhythm written in a circle.

As can be seen, the count is marked where to begin the rhythm, in this case on 8, signified by the 0 figure – and reading clockwise, the rhythm can be seen to be that of the shim sham: 8 and 1, 2 and 3, 4 and 5 and 6 and 7, using the shuffle step-written previously above. *See* the shim sham section above.

There is one circle for each eight counts, and they can be read across and labelled as necessary to give continuity. In this way I believe the clock to be a shorthand to writing down rhythm, which in itself can be laborious and indeed sometimes confusing. If the rhythm or sound can be 'seen by diagram', it just may be the key to getting students to enjoy counting; though in younger dancers this can prove to be a problem, even though we are only dealing with just eight numbers! I encourage the reader to try this unique method at the earliest opportunity, and practise looking at the diagram to become familiar with it.

As an example, we can use the whole of the shim sham first part written as a circle:

Compare this diagrammatical idea to the text of the steps above. They are the same, of course, but it's easy to see that the clock idea is a good short-hand and quickly absorbed.

Now it is possible to see the whole phase of four bars of the shim sham, and all are counted in the same way, beginning on the figure 0 and counting round, with due care to the spaces between the numbers. Read only where the circle is marked with the line, and only say where this mark falls. If a number is missed out we don't need to say it. For example, in the shim sham break this reads 8 1 2 3 and and 5 6 7. There is no count of 4 because we have syncopated it out; *although it is there as our tempo, it is not part of our rhythm*.

Let us see if we can stretch our minds to putting down all of the four shim sham parts in this rhythm clock fashion. Take the time to gain familiarity with it, and it will all become easier.

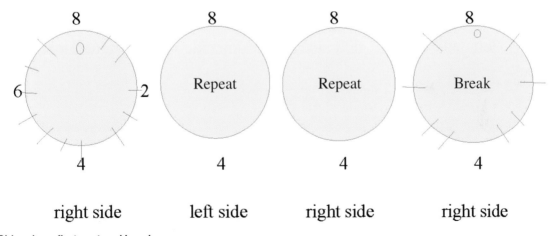

right side   left side   right side   right side

Shim sham first part and break.

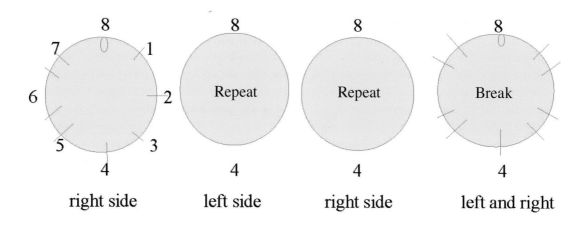

Shim sham Cross-Over and break.

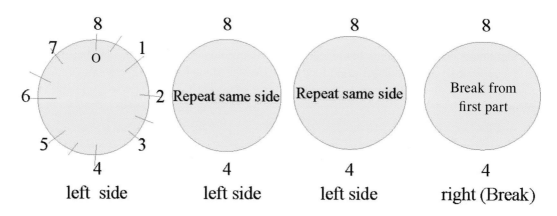

Shim sham Tack Annie and break.

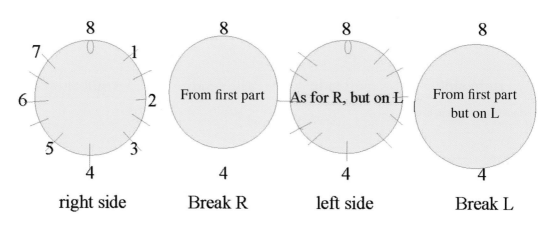

Shim sham Falling Off a Log and break.

Reading an amalgamation is not easy for some, and of course if we can't see this sound it doesn't mean we can't tap dance. I have only used the cross-over and break in picture form here. Tap is, after all, for the benefit of the ears predominantly, and in some styles this is the entire point, in rhythm tap.

Learning a tap dance routine is again about practice, and although people practise elements such as shuffles and hops, then bars of these elements, followed by connecting those bars together in a continuous fashion, *dancing* them is a special and separate art in itself. Students are often heard in the classroom saying 'I know each part, but I can't put them together'. It's that ABC thing again, and the constructing of short 'words', longer words and 'sentences', and so on.

We are getting close to dancing at this stage, but dancing takes us to a place beyond technique, and beyond thought too, in some ways. This is where advanced technique is required, and the only way to achieve an advanced way with all the elements comes with constant practice.

CHAPTER 6

ADVANCED TECHNIQUE

The first thing that needs to be addressed is, what is meant by advanced technique? Is it speed or is it clarity? Is it learning so-called harder figures to do? Is it a multitude of rhythms, or is it dexterity with the feet? Or can it be clever with music, using different genres? Does the footwork doing tricks and odd things make it 'better' or more advanced? What is advanced, anyway? As with all art, it should not be judged but just appreciated, thereby taking it out of the context of competition, when the more difficult things are judged 'advanced' simply because they are 'harder'. Which is best, an apple or an orange?

In tap dance we can say with certainty a few things about this state called advanced. One is that *clarity* has to be counted as advanced, and two, that *musicality* has to be counted as advanced – and even *artistry* has a place too, of course. Get these few things right, and we are at least on the way to being called advanced – and it doesn't have to be because the steps have the tag marked 'harder' attached. In considering musicality the advanced tap dancer will use the idea of something called 'cross phrasing', and will come up with quite amazing results if it is mastered properly. Let us have another definition here to be clear about this:

Cross phrasing: is when the dancer's phrase crosses the music phrase.

To explain, the music can be in, say, a standard 4/4 (with four beats to the bar, four bars to the phrase) but the figure the dancer is doing could be in, say, 3 counts *before it repeats*. This is a vital aspect of

the idea of advanced technique, and what we can do further with our two feet and our rudiments already learned. The dancer doing the figure which takes 3 counts but to the music taking 4 counts will produce a figure that, every time it's repeated, will sound different because it will start on a different count and will not coincide. Counted like this below it hopefully makes sense to the reader:

Beginning the dancer's 3-count phrase on 1, say: 1 2 3, but the next time the dancer does the figure he will begin on 4 in the music and will end on 2. Here we can see that he has done his figure four times *but* has used three bars of music:

1 2 3; <u>4</u> / 1 2; <u>3</u> 4 / 1; <u>2</u> 3 4

We can do this again with, say, 7 counts to repeat the dancer's figure and the music is in 4/4 as follows, beginning his counts on the underlined number:

<u>1</u> 2 3 4 / 1 2 3 <u>4</u> / 1 2 3 4 /
1 2 <u>3</u> 4 / 1 2 3 4 1 <u>2</u>

The first 7 counts is 1 ..... 3; the second is from 4 ..... 2; the third is from 3 ......1. This gives the impression that the dancer is doing much more than he actually is, because it sounds 'wrong' to the ear, but in fact is clever and innovative. By doing a simple thing like repeating in his head, he can cross the phrase because the numbers 4 (music counts to the bar) and 7 (dancer's counts) do not match and he sounds much cleverer because of this simple idea of doing the same thing but sounding different every time.

THE ADVANCED DANCER

Having a catalogue of steps at our toe tips and in the head, or in the soul as it were, surely must rate alongside that of the pianist who can reproduce a classical piece at a performance without a sheet of music in front of them. This kind of memory is extraordinary and I think cannot be learned by just anyone; I believe it to be a natural talent, but that it can be helped by nurturing.

It is the same with the advanced tap dancer, who is, as we have discussed so far in this book, a musician and a percussionist. Again, without a sheet of music to look at or a book to glance over, the advanced tap dancer will be a performer as well as a great technician. He or she will simply not need to look anywhere other than to their inner instincts when dancing. As already stated, this fits well with the jazz musician's own innate sense of freedom, and it is worth repeating that as tap is an original jazz dance, it only stands to reason that the spontaneous aspect is probably no less than essential to the advanced dancer.

As with anything, the art of practice will achieve an advanced state, and in tap dancing this isn't possible without the kind of mindset that requires the feet to react instantaneously to the demands of the brain when dancing full out and at speed. Indeed at these moments it is vital not to think at all. Having the more difficult steps as part of our catalogue in the brain obviously plays a great part.

Looking at advanced technique in the syllabus world, it means acquiring ever more convoluted and contrived steps to be able to don that label. Having an advanced technique will not in itself make an advanced dancer – rather, it will just make an advanced technician. Musicality will not just come along with going faster or with a more 'difficult' invention with a shuffle or a new way with an old idea. These things are all right in themselves, but just forever inventing so-called 'new' things is not being advanced in the true sense; it is actually making the fence higher to jump over and calling it better. It is better in sporting dialogue, but real *dancing* is not a sport or a competition. Perhaps a definition would help here?

An advanced technique: will help the tap dancer to go further, but he/she will need to demonstrate much else besides, such as musicality, clarity and tonality.

Musicality, clarity and tonality are surely what the truly advanced dancer is aiming for. Tonality will be the product of long experience and exhausting practice and obviously much searching for perfection. Few achieve this state, but even that is purely subjective, after all. Everyone has an opinion on what is advanced or is perfect, but what is certain is that desire and practice and dedication are absolutely key to achieving advanced ability.

Here we could attempt to describe endlessly complex steps and figures in order to have a try at achieving them; but that is difficult and almost impossible to see just with photographs and without a recorded action on a DVD or a film. Far better, I think, to describe *what it takes* to become advanced using so-called advanced steps and ideas, but to include the things I have stated above in order to achieve this level of ability. The end result with the harder or more advanced step has to be enhanced by these other qualities, or we are only dancing the technique – and that is not really dancing. I guess what I am saying is, gaining ever more so-called difficult steps is not necessarily producing an advanced dancer, and could actually get in the way.

The teacher with experience will immediately recognize the supposedly advanced tapper coming into the studio, and will perhaps groan slightly because they know such students can be among the weakest dancers of this genre. Too much technique has blinded them to what's important, and they simply cannot find the *dance* in themselves (though this doesn't apply to all of them, of course): they have sacrificed musicality, form, line, clarity and *fun* for the dubious honour of more technique. In fact they can be quite boring to watch! Straining to do certain advanced steps can be unattractive, and counts for not very much.

ADVANCED TAP DANCE FIGURES

This section begins with a list of what are considered to be advanced tap figures; these are then described, and finally are put into a routine that could be said to be advanced. Remember that complexity is in the eye (and ear) of the beholder, and some 'advanced tappers' may not even consider the following figures advanced any more, now that they have been mastered so completely! Nevertheless it is *how* they have been mastered and are *used* from then on that awards the status.

The list of what are considered to be advanced tap figures is as follows:

- Flaps
- Three-beat shuffles
- Three-beat shuffles in time steps
- Quicker and smaller pick-ups; double pick-ups
- Double pick-ups in time steps
- Double flaps
- Paddles in 3, 4 and 5; paddles in time steps
- Riffs in 3, 4, 5, 6, 7 and so on

- Cramp rolls
- Toe stands
- Wings

Although some of the following have already been mentioned, they nevertheless must be described again if we are to have a series of advanced steps. Thus the advanced figures are described below in detail.

Flaps

Flaps are quicker and brighter tap steps, and are thus shorter in execution. Mentioned earlier as a basic tap step, they are done with the knee lifted and in a strong downward movement, and not so much of a forward movement. They appear to be as if the dancer is marching with a straightened knee on landing, and they are very definitely an American way, with a simple but essential step. Because of the shorter and quicker action they will give the dancer much greater speed and a better look. Traditionally they have always been done this way in the USA, and in shows such as *42nd St* it is the required foot action. They can be stationary or they can travel.

Flaps (Tap Steps). **1. Prepare to lift the R foot...**

2. ...lift the leg up and in front with a flexed ankle...

3. ...strike the foot hard and crisply into the floor, and with an instantaneous lift of the other leg on the weight change.

Three-Beat Shuffles

The three-beat shuffle uses the heel and toe in a 'toe-heel-toe' brushing action, and not the usual 'toe toe' brushing action. It is counted as 'and a 1'. The dancer is doing both a shuffle and a paddle *at the same time* to produce a more interesting sound.

Three-Beat Shuffles in the Time Step

If we add the three-beat shuffle into an established step such as our traditional time step we are embellishing it and can say it is then more advanced. For instance, taking a single time step, and instead of the normal shuffle, we can use the three-beat shuffle and can do a pick-up within the time step too.

An example would be thus: a single time step on the R, with a three-beat shuffle, using a pick-up instead of the hop, and beginning on the count of 8. Count it like so:

8 and and a 1, 2 and 3 and (R);
4 and and a 5, 6 and 7 and (L).

The first count after the 8 is a *sixteenth* note, and the others are either *quarter* notes or *eighth* notes.

Pick-Ups and Double Pick-Ups

Pick-ups are performed either on the ball of the foot going backwards, or by letting the foot naturally roll down to the heel as the dancer advances backwards. The latter frees the hips and allows the dancer to roll the step back to give a more jazz-based look. Doing normal pick-ups going backwards on the ball of the foot constantly can lead to a stiff-looking gait, but some dancers prefer this method.

Double pick-ups are also called 'double pull-backs', because the dancer pulls back and up, either from the ball of the foot or from a flat foot, to land a short distance behind. Having done, in order, pick-up, pick-up, land, land, this is an air step and needs elevation, so the knees have to bend in preparation to springing up and backwards.

Double Pick-up.   1. Say 'and and a 1' (a sixteenth note) Pk-up, Pk-up, transfer transfer: standing in both feet on the ball of foot, knees flexed...

2. ...ready to spring backwards, then...

3. ...strike the toe tap on the L backwards and up...

4. ...land onto the ball of the foot on the R then the L.

Using the *sixteenth* note it sounds like 'and and a 1'. This is a very quick action and produces four sounds in one count. To learn this the dancer has to adjust the distance travelled and the amount of lift required to close down this rhythm – a difficult thing for the beginner, but well used for the advanced tap dancer. A further advance on this would be achieved if the dancer then dropped the heels in quick succession to produce *six sounds*!

Double Pick-Ups in Time Steps
These steps are a good replacement for the shuffle and the hop. With the weight in the left foot do a stomp on the right, followed by a pick-up on the right, then immediately a pick-up on the left landing on the left. Count it thus: 1 and a 2, 3 and 4 and; 5 and a 6, 7 and 8 and.

Double Flaps
The dancer needs to get up off the floor and from one foot spring forwards to do a flap on both feet, one a split second before the other. This is an air step and needs elevation to succeed. It is again

counted as 'and and a 1', the sixteenth note. If the reader were to assume that this is the direct opposite of the previous double pull-back, then he or she would be correct to do so.

Paddles in 3, 4 and 5; Paddles in Time Steps

A paddle is a double sound like the shuffle, but is done with the heel and toe, and not the toe and toe brush action of the shuffle. The heel is a downward dig into the floor at the point of where the working leg is extended, and then by pulling the foot back, the toe is struck as in a pick-up. In this way it is exactly as a shuffle, but a great deal quicker because it is lower.

When the foot lands after the paddle it is now a three-beat sound and thus a 'paddle step' *or* a 'three-beat paddle' (this is an easier way to remember it). Adding the heel after this we can now call it a 'four-beat paddle', and it is now a heel dig, a pick-up, a weight change on to the ball, and a heel beat – all on the same foot, of course. This produces a super-fast *sixteenth* note, and to the advanced dancer, paddles are the most important thing in his or her tap repertoire (refer back to the figures in the pictures above).

Going further, if we then add to this to achieve five beats we will need a heel after the first two sounds and before the last two sounds. This should be read as: paddle R, heel L, ball R, heel R, and should be counted thus: a 1 and a 2, a 3 and a 4 and going from one foot to the other.

Five-beat paddles, having five sounds, are great

for cross-phrasing and rhythm changes because the odd number of sounds does not go into either a 2 or a 4 or an 8 count of reference. A five-beat paddle is therefore a very useful thing to do.

Paddles in time steps: Described simply, this would be just to replace the shuffles with paddles everywhere. Because paddles keep the feet low and are much quicker, all of the time steps, traditional or otherwise, are going to look more relaxed and can be executed at super speed.

Riffs in 3, 4, 5, 6, 7

Riffs are basically walking steps that allow the dancer to stride and change weight with a range of sounds instead of just one or two or three. They form a quick movement with multi sounds of between three and seven beats, and get the dancer to progress from the spot. They can be done without travelling, but are more effective when they do travel.

Raise the foot behind and brush forwards with the toe, then land the heel down, bringing a full foot down to produce three sounds: one in the air, and two on the floor. I would call this a three-beat riff, and it travels. However, if we do a brush with the toe and a brush with the heel, then followed by a heel beat on the other foot, we also get three sounds but we have not moved from the spot: another kind of three-beat riff.

To do multi riffs the dancer can do this three-beat stationary riff both forwards and then backwards (working leg riffs forwards, then bring back catching the heel, followed by a toe brush back, then a heel beat on the other foot). This can be done as many times as the dancer wishes before finishing with, say, a five-beat riff. In this way as many sounds as desired are produced – even a thirty-two-beat riff is possible!

A four-beat riff is as follows: a brush forwards with the toe, a brush forwards with the heel, a heel beat landing, a full toe beat on the spot, or slightly travelled in one step and all with the same foot.

A five-beat riff is the same, but with another heel from the other foot added into the middle of the above.

NOTE

Remember, this one action called a paddle is a fundamental and essential component of rhythm tap, and if the reader cares to watch Fred Astaire himself, he will see he uses more paddles than shuffles in all his films!

3-Beat Riff Fwd. 1. Say 'toe heel-heel' on the R stationary... pull the foot back and up...

2. ...toe brush to forwards, followed by heel brush forwards...

3. ...heel beat on the other foot.

3-Beat Riff Bkwd. 1. Say 'heel toe heel' on the R stationary... leg is lifted in front...

2. ...heel brush backwards, followed by toe brush backwards...

3. ...heel beat on the other foot.

4-Beat Riff.   1. Say: 'toe heel heel toe' on the R travelling... bring leg back...

2. ...toe brush forwards...

3. ...followed by heel brush forwards...

4. ...brush through off the floor, leg extended fully...

5. ...return heel to the floor...

6. ...toe beat down, bend the knee, change weight into the foot.

5-Beat Riff.   1. Say 'toe heel heel heel toe', emphasize the heel on L travelling... prepare to lift the leg back and up...

2. ...lift leg back...

3. ...toe brush forwards...

4. ...followed by heel brush forwards...

5. ...heel beat into the floor on L...

6. ...return heel to the floor...

7. ...toe beat down, bend the knee, change weight
into the foot.

Cramp Roll.   1. Say 'and and a 1' (a sixteenth note).
Ball ball, heel heel... standing on the ball of both feet,
knees flexed slightly...

2. ...in this case, the right foot beats first slightly forwards on the ball...

3. ...followed by the left beating into line with the right...

4. ...the heel of the right beats into the floor with a change of weight...

5. ...the heel of the left beats into line with the right foot.

The six-beat riff is the above, but with a heel beat on the same foot added on to the end. The seven-beat riff is the five-beat riff with two heel beats added at the end (on the back foot, then the front foot). This ensures the whole thing has the last sound, and thus the change of weight, on the working foot. This is both a travelling and a single stride executed step.

Riffs can be counted in various ways and according to the imagination of the dancer. They are often taught in only one rhythm, but are much more flexible.

Cramp Rolls

Cramp rolls are executed like so: ball beat R, ball beat L, heel beat R, heel beat L. This is a fast *sixteenth* note sound and has to be done, as the name suggests, as if cramping together four sounds into one count. Bend the knees, and as if pressing the feet into the floor, do a four-beat cramp roll. For a five-beat cramp roll do a flap first on the R, the ball on the left, then heel beat R, heel beat L. Count: a1 and a 2.

Toe Stands

Toe stands are an old invention: since as far back as the 1920s in America girl tappers were doing whole routines on pointe, the toe taps on the very end of the shoes! This was always somewhat of a novelty, and didn't become a mainstream action for tap dancers. More recently dancers are elevating on to the toes for a split second and producing an exciting-looking featured step and again producing a *sixteenth* note sound, the same as the cramp roll and the double pull-back.

Wings

Wings are the same sort of step as toe stands, but were adopted into the mainstream lexicon of steps, and many artists from history have used them. The Condos Brothers are credited with inventing this air step, and they were phenomenal in their execution at super speed with a veritable blizzard of wings in their act and on film. Used sparingly they are an attractive step; however, doing double wings (on both feet) with the added feature of the winging or

Toe Stand.   1. Say 'and and a 1' (a sixteenth note) toe toe, step step… bend both knees and prepare to jump up…

2. …using the arms to jump up will help with the lift from the floor…

3. …(at this instant the dancer is in the air)…

4. …strike the toe point, first R, then L, into the floor speedily. The weight changes on both…

5. …land on the balls of the foot first R, then L, bending the knees.

'flying' arms they can look particularly amateur, and the modern advanced tap dancer will almost never be found using them in this way.

Wings on the one foot are a better and a harder option, and dancers from history such as Gene Kelly and Gene Nelson make these advanced elements look sublime.

To do them on both feet (double wings) the weight is first evenly placed on the balls of both feet. Lifting off from the floor and scraping the outside edge of the shoe out to the side, the dancer needs to lift off just as much as it takes to maintain contact with the floor when jumping into the air. Then the feet have to return in place.

Bringing back the feet together, the tap is now struck on to the floor to give an inward sound before landing on to the balls of both feet after the tap strikes the floor. There are three sounds here, on both feet: the first is the outward swishing sound and the other two are the same as the pick-up step, *but inwards*.

Wings–Double.   1. Say 'and a 1' for each foot simultaneously... weight on both feet, preparing to spring off the floor...

2. ...as the body lifts up and the knees straighten, the ankles need to slide outwards on the outside edge of the shoes to produce a light sound...

3. ...the returning sound is a catch inwards with the toe tap-dancing...

4. ...the last sound is the landing on both feet together.

Doing the wing on one foot it is as above, but with one leg lifted in front with a bent knee, and the other doing what has just been described.

Wings take a great deal of practice and patience, and can be a good-looking feature when mastered. Within a dance piece they are very effective if used sparingly and imaginatively. They are most impressive when they are unexpectedly slotted into a fast-paced routine and act like a flash of brilliance in the action. This kind of imagination is advanced technique.

To give a typical advance routine credence we need to bear in mind the other enhancements detailed above. If we can do that, we are becoming an advanced dancer and one we would like to watch. The tap dancer Claire Hitchman's idea of what would constitute an advanced routine is as follows: '…intricate rhythms; changes of speed; clever musicality; other dance aspects and borrowing from, say, Latin and not just footwork; presentation and an overall polish' – and I agree.

ADVANCED TAP ROUTINE

Using some of the above advanced tap elements, we will attempt to do a typical advanced tap routine via the written word. Good luck!

Music: A good and lively pace in a swing rhythm style.

Steps:

A. Flap R flap L, 5 beat riff on the R out to the R side;
    a1 a2 a3 and a 4

B. Shuffle ball change L to R, with weight fully into the R foot
    a5 a6

C. Spring on to L and bring R in towards the L, and using as in a fouette action, do a spring and single turn on the L, landing the feet down R L R
    7   8   1 2 3. (The count for the turn will take
    7   8)

D. Pause on 4

E. You are now on the R; pk-up stp L, ball change R L; pk-up stp R ball change L R
    and 5 and 6 and 7 and 8

F. Spring on to L and do a three-beat static riff with the R, both forward and back
    1 and a 2 and a 3

G. Shuffle R heel L step R
    and and a 4

H. Ball-heel L R L R L R , stamp L
    5 and and a 6 and and a 7 and and a 8 (very fast-paced ball-heels and in double time, sixteenth notes again)

I. Three-beat shuffle on the R ball change R L; repeat this on the R; stomp R on an accent 'and'
    1 and and a 2   3 and and a 4   and
    'grapevine' (running step) to the R side
    using L R L R L R
    and 6   and 7   and 8 using alternate step positions beginning L behind R

J. Repeat I. as above on the L using the same counting

K. Forward cramp roll on the R and and a 1; step step spring R L R in place 2   3   4
    Step in to the L and do a wing on this foot; do a three-beat shuffle on the R, step R, stamp L; 5 and a 6 7 and and a 8

This is a typical high speed amalgamation and not too difficult; after being tried a few times it will develop quickly into a neater version of itself. Although only five bars of eight counts, it is enough to see that the use of the advanced figures does play a part, and the added elements of a performance quality and musicality will serve to give it a reasonable level of difficulty. It has syncopation and a change of timing, as all tap pieces should have.

Advanced technique will aid all further things in tap dance, and the dancer will then achieve a good status that can be called advanced. No matter how many advanced steps are 'invented', they will mean little if the dancer then fails to give it all an advanced look and an advanced quality, which leads to a professional performance. The most vital thing is in the *using* of the advanced elements, and the actual putting together of the music and steps. The dancer who cannot see, or rather hear, the passages in the music that will lend themselves to the routine, such as a quiet section or a tacet section, is not as advanced as he or she could be. Ignoring these characteristics is to ignore the musicality itself.

Finally, in my own considered opinion, the true advanced dancer is the one who can instantly adjust to or, shall we say, 'choose' the steps that *match perfectly the music he or she is hearing*. The jazz tap dancer's prized goal is surely intuition in the execution, which happens to be the jazz musician's goal also.

CHAPTER 7

PROFESSIONAL DEVELOPMENT

We should here look at two ways to go forwards, the professional way and the amateur way, because there are easily more amateur tap dancers around than professional tap dancers. The general public is huge in number and many classes up and down the country have large attendances. Perhaps an alternative title here will serve as a heading for progressing with learning to tap. I don't know, but in any case the amateur state obviously precedes the other more elevated status. If the learner has been bitten by the 'tap bug' he or she may want to do as much as they can to further their individual passion and then become professional.

THE ESTABLISHED PATH

Providing someone wants to be a professional dancer and wants to go through the often gruelling but rewarding hours of constant practice, strained and pulled muscles, long hours in pain from stretching, endless risk of injury, and without any guarantees, whether it be ballet or jazz dance or tap, and is aware of the fact that many dancers will have limited success, they will at least benefit from being super fit at the end of training!

I will begin this section by considering the end result of professional development.

There are professional solo tap dancers around, of course, but unless they have something different to add to the genre they will probably have at best a moderate career. There are rarely calls for solo tap dancers in the mainstream, but where the well versed in all things tap dance congregate, there are roads to success. Of the tap *groups* that have existed, certainly since the early 1980s, the

majority of them are from America, the place where dance and particularly tap dance is valued and even revered. America cherishes its dancers where other countries just have them, and this is demonstrated in the aspect of *funding*. Funding for the arts is a delicate subject in many countries, but the USA seems to be the place where it is mostly to be found, and in dance particularly, I am informed.

When a dance company is seeking sponsorship and can demonstrate that it definitely has something different to say on the subject, it will attract funding (it is to be hoped). The alternative for the tap dance company is long periods of no work followed by small gigs in small venues and usually for an already converted audience; essentially it has a minority appeal. It depends a lot on the location and the country.

Dance is well recognized as the Cinderella of the arts world, and the effort that goes into the training is out of proportion to the work gained that earns the money from it as a professional. The old way a solo tap performer could earn money from dancing as a viable living was as a 'song and dance man' type of act. This act always needed a venue where they staged 'review'-type entertainment – and this is harking back to the days of on-the-road touring, with all its dubious attractions! Even today, hotels and clubs and pubs do not always have the luxury of a stage or a floor, and certainly the old-style venues could be fairly rough-and-ready places to earn that meagre fee.

This solo performer would have had his own sheet music, and would have to hope there was a competent pianist at the venue as well as a decent floor on which to dance. More alarmingly, many venues

Look for shoes with a particularly large build-up of leather under the tap, giving a lot of 'help' to the dancer with the added volume this feature brings.

would have been carpeted, either on stage or even on the floor, because the sorts of act that predominated in clubs and pubs were not dance acts, but more likely involved artists who sang or played an instrument or were comedians.

The present-day solo tapper in the more up-to-date venue will have a pre-recorded soundtrack to bring along and use; but he or she would still need a good floor and a good PA system. He or she will perhaps be known and be part of a dance show that is either all tappers, or perhaps are on the bill as guest artists. Often these tap dancers will be invited to teach as part of a festival of dance, and in this way will build a reputation as a performer of merit. This artist will only be as good as their previous appearance, and success will depend on their skill with their technique, their catalogue of moves and their clarity, as well as their skilful audience manipulation. This is a given, but is not always achievable.

The newer way forward to the dream of success in tap dancing is as part of a group that will also tour, and which will have a much better chance of success, not least from being more than one pair of shoes making the sounds. Again, these types of act are found mostly in America, and are generally welcomed as part of an arts weekend or a special dance occasion. Tap-dancing stars are of course around, but it is the dedicated and immensely focused and passionate person who will be successful.

Now to return to the beginning.

THE ROUTE TO PROFESSIONALISM

So how have these particular dancers developed? What do they have that makes them superior in tap dancing that the serious amateur does not have? Is it the training, or the opportunity, or the pure dedication and desire that brings their success? Do they have a uniquely natural talent and the good fortune to be seen in their pursuit to the top?

The answer is in all of these, and in their own personal history. A typical route to the top of the tree in tap dancing begins in a dance school, whether local or in an acclaimed school for an arts vocation, and the person who finds that tap dance has become their favourite form of dance is the one who will noticeably develop quicker in it and with little effort. It will seem almost easy to them, and the sharp-eyed teacher will perhaps help that young dancer more readily. It will be the same if they were into ballet or jazz dance. In any dance school the naturally talented will shine through pretty quickly.

To be able to tap dance well does not necessarily mean the dancer has to do well in other forms of dance; it is quite possible to specialize in one thing only, and this is true with all dance genres. If that person goes on to be a solo artist, and develops their dance as a speciality, they will actually need to be this singularly focused. Tap dancers are specialists because they are also musicians in the form of percussionists. A common thing found in the dance world is that ballet and tap are as oil and water, but there are exceptions.

The Professional Training Establishment

The next stage in the development of becoming a tap dancer (and a dancer) is the stage academy or the professional training establishment that exists in many cities and in some countries. To be part of the 'dance community' is for some a dream occupation, and the training for it a perfect way towards working for a living. Based as it is on eternal hope as well as ideals, dancing to earn a living and be paid a wage at the end of the week is for some the ultimate goal. It is an attractive proposition, and a deceptively hard one to carry out if the intrinsic desire and drive are weak.

These performing arts institutions at Further Education level take on students from the age of about sixteen to twenty-one, and usually offer a three-year training course in *all* the performing arts. This is to deliver an all-round training, and to try to ensure a better chance of employment at the end of the course. To get into such a place an audition is the usual route, along with any specialist accomplishments the student can demonstrate, such as guitar or piano playing. Predominantly, though, singing and dancing are key, followed by acting or drama experience.

Within this period the student will hopefully gain enough confidence and ability to go on and progress to a professional level, and thus earn a living as a performer. The crucial factor that students of the performing arts need to identify is exactly what their strengths are, and then to play to them. Having an all-round training is very good, but a specialism gives that extra chance in the working world. So it is with tap dance, and to concentrate on becoming a solo tap dancer in what is a niche market, the student will merely use other dance disciplines as vehicles to help with their passion for tap.

This is of course, a road of choice. Within the academy situation all things are on the menu, and in the main, tap dance will be approached equally with all other dance forms. The training for a career in dance itself comes first, with any specialisms carried along with this training. The students will learn to get used to a day with a timetable and a structure, and a typical day in such a college may look something like the table on page 108.

The college would endeavour to give as much training/teaching deemed essential for a career in the performing arts, and the destinations upon graduating would be anything from local independent dance or theatre companies to full-blown ballet companies or cruise ship open auditions.

A college course such as just described would be of the utmost advantage in this latter destination because this kind of training suits the all-round requirements of the cruise ship entertainment schedule. Each day in the college would be different, with perhaps the ballet classes occurring three days a week, because traditionally ballet is considered to be the mainstay of a dancer's training, building on core strength and muscle toning.

The teachers are hired by the college, usually on reputation gained in the business themselves. Sometimes they are required to have a specific qualification in their subject in order to give the students the chance to also gain recognized exam status as part of their course. There are a number of dance associations in the UK providing exams, and all offer extensive courses in all dance subjects. Within these associations the young learner can go quite far into the world of dance. Academy courses can also be tailored to students' needs and abilities.

This kind of college environment has a professional developmental process, and should be well worth the two or three years spent in attending. As

A Typical Day in a Performing Arts Institution

Day	Time	Class/year	Location
Monday	8.30–9.45	Ballet. All years Olivia H	Studio A
	10.00–11.15	Tap/singing groups: First year/third year Fred A/Frank S	Studio B /rec studio
	10.00–11.15	Jazz: Second year Bob F	Studio A
	11.30–1.00	Acting/tap: second year/ third year Jazz: first year Jonny D./Donald O. Bob F	Theatre/studio Studio A
	1.00–1.45	LUNCH	
	1.45–3.00	Jazz /ballet pas de deux. Third year/all second year boys, first year girls Singing groups second year girls Luigi/Mikhail B Vera L	Studio A for jazz Studio B for ballet Theatre for singing
	3.15–5.15	Jazz pas de deux/singing groups All third year boys, second year girls/first year Luigi/Vera L	Studio A Theatre
	5.15–6.30	Rehearsal summer show. All years Principal Mrs T	Theatre

with all further education, a lot of the study is left to the individual student and their own particular desires and ambitions. Any good teacher or coach will tell the student that nobody can teach them to dance: they can only show the student what to do. The rest is up to the individual and their own personal quest for excellence. Dancing for a living is not an easy thing to do, but all training, if taken seriously, should help oil the wheels. Any college is only as good as its teachers.

Looking at the 'tongue in cheek' timetable above, tap dance would form just one part of the training, and it would be up to the student after they leave the course of study to pursue any specialism they feel they can. This 'after training' is probably the only way that someone with a good and innate tap dance skill will progress – namely to carry on with it after leaving, taking private lessons from well-known tap dancers and teachers who have travelled the path themselves, and by practising exhaustively and constantly to hone a performance level skill. This personal quest is what would have to happen with any other instrument.

If we can imagine the path of the aspiring solo tap dance performer we must assume that he or she will look for those professional performers and teachers who are in the business of teaching and passing on the steps and moves and ideas that they themselves learned on their own journey. They will look for opportunities to go along to a workshop or a performance, and seek to better themselves in this way.

The other way will be harder (or easier, depending on the person), and that will be the way of the fiercely independent individual who thinks they will teach themselves, since to do so will ensure they are the sole master of their style and their way with rhythm. For this person the path to glory as a dance specialist in tap is probably more rewarding because all the work will be from themselves and by themselves; that seems suspiciously like the old days of American Broadway when artists such as the Nicholas Brothers and John Bubbles were busy doing it for themselves.

It is true that nobody can teach anyone *actually* to dance. All bodies are different (thank goodness), and all bodies respond in different ways to different stimuli. Only by passing down such a quantity of knowledge through the years and decades have such things as improvement in ability and technique survived. How else can anything go into the future and go on to inspire endlessly? Books will not do it, nor will film clips on the internet, but stories and anecdotes and actual living performances will do more than anything to influence the next generation.

Performers who turn to teaching are going to be better at producing other performers and tap dance stars, and no amount of reading or passing of exams is going to compare to the one-to-one approach of learning to dance *from the person*. Dance is a living thing and has to be seen, heard and felt. Real tap dance can only be passed on by being present with another person, and one with a proven talent for the subject. The great and wonderful tap artists have now all passed on, and all we are left with is their appearances on film, which are simply marvellous. But we cannot be in the presence of greatness any more because tap on that level is gone. However, we have other great tappers coming along, such as Evan Ruggiero (*see* Chapter 1), and following people such as this will be the way.

THE AMATEUR WAY

For the dancer wanting to be better at tap dance but not wanting the status of professional performer, the exam or syllabus system is going to be the ideal starting point for instilling into the learner the sort of discipline that will improve them. Just because the professional status is not wanted it still can be sought after with professional development. Seeking out the teachers who are adept at this kind of teaching and style is not difficult, since all towns and cities will most likely have dance schools that cater for all ages; most of these schools will offer some exam-type classes, which can be followed as far as the learner desires to go.

However, going along as an adult to these places can be a daunting prospect since the school will be mostly full of children, with any adult class just an

Dancing as a couple requires great attention to detail if the dancers want to mirror each other. The alternative is perhaps more adventurous when they complement each other, and allow for individual personality to shine through in performance.

after-hours addition. Some syllabus systems say that they cater for the adult within their exam structure by offering bronze, silver and gold medal tests, but really what is needed is the ex-professional teacher or performer who needs the extra money and lives close by and is giving private lessons. Otherwise the basics will be taught and learned, and that will be as far as it goes.

Dance centres have this further level of teacher and practising professionals, in all disciplines, and contained in them can be found a great menu of dance, and the teachers that teach them. The classes are also self-regulating, because quite simply if the teacher is not up to the job, the paying customer will not return and the class will close. Centres such as these are either just studio-letting facilities, or they operate on a split fee basis; this fact is irrelevant to the customer, who wants to learn to dance – and why should it matter? The paying customer is only wanting value for money.

Aside from an open class there is the private lesson, which can be quite expensive – the professional teacher will set his or her prices, to include a studio fee. Suppose the amateur dancer is at a certain stage of excellence and wants to revitalize their own technique and their own steps, and even seek new ways to progress. This dancer will be looking for so-called 'newer' things to do. But the truth is, there are few 'new' things to do, and the advanced dancer will be on a quest for improvement within their own personality and musical capabilities.

The path of the solo dancer trying to earn a living will be better if they can establish a reputation so that other dancers will come along and learn from them. This is today the same as it always was, in that people take from other people, the main difference compared to when I was learning being that there are now short cuts on various media outlets. However, nothing can compare to being in the presence of an individual dancer/teacher/choreographer in a studio alone with tap shoes.

In the far-off days of the Cotton Club in New York's Harlem, in the early years of tap dance around the 1920s and 1930s, this practice of taking from those who put themselves forward as teachers was the way to learn. Going along to see a show or a performer was both an occasion and a quest, but remembering what they saw afterwards was the trick to be mastered. It is more likely that the budding professional will prefer to do things their own way, since to laboriously copy and borrow from great dancers on film or video is hard work, and actually harder to do than explore within the self.

Tap dancing is very personal, and as personal as the voice of the individual. They should seek to improve on this level after first gaining as much information as they can from open classes or exam syllabuses. As I have said, nobody can teach you how to dance because it is your body and it rests with you. The soloist will want to develop a style of their own, to say something different, to put their own spin on their dancing.

So for the amateur adult dancer, the open class is the best way forwards. The dance centre will have tap classes at various levels and with various teachers, and the student will come to realize which class and which teacher is the one for them. Something will click for them when that teacher is found, and soon after the serious student will start to find their own way; even more, if they have that desire to practise all Sunday afternoon in their own home, or even in the garden on their own little bit of board, they will improve.

We are all human, and we know our bodies and capabilities better than anyone, and the practice instinct is either powerful or it isn't. Either way, this is what will bring the most joy as we strive to get it right and clear. When we know we have a talent we all want to see just how far we can go with it. In dance, this striving is particularly strong, and this is easily understood because it is a natural thing. The fact that it is allied with a certain style of music that is also seemingly natural with the body – that is, jazz music – is a distinct bonus, and it is no accident that tap and jazz grew up together.

That is why tap dance is so great. It is of the folk themselves, and as such it will always survive, in some way, in some body, in some place. Although the truly talented old guard has left the scene, there will be others to seek out and learn from.

CHAPTER 8

FITNESS AND TRAINING

What will tap dance require of us when we begin to learn it for the first time? What will it require when we reach an advanced stage? What do we need in terms of fitness, in order to dance any style? How will our fitness affect our training? Tap dancing in the first stages of learning is virtually a static thing, with the basics being practised on the spot first, and then moved about if that is the style desired. Learning to dance as a young person is very different to learning to dance as an adult, and apart from the obvious, such as embarrassment and feelings of physical shortcoming, the adult learner will be focused on the brain being fit enough to take on board complex instructions for the body to deal with.

DO WE NEED EXTREME FITNESS?

We have to have an *aptitude* and an approach to learning similar to that for a physical sport. There is a difference, in that dancing is not a physically dangerous sport such as rugby or boxing, but nevertheless it can be risky and potentially harmful to do some dance styles. Ballet, for instance, belies its wonderfully aesthetic looks when seen on stage, but in cold fact, the leaps and lifts and the risk of injury to limb and lower back are never far away. In tap dance it is not this bad, but even in, say, a mix of tap and hip hop, some moves are attempted that could be said to be injury inducing. In this case it would depend on the dancer and the amount of risk he wishes to put on himself. Also, street dances are literally *on the street*, and that means concrete or worse, so the knees are highly susceptible to injury.

It is well worth looking on the internet for a few black and white movies of the Nicholas Brothers or the Berry Brothers to see just how far they were prepared to push their bodies. These iconic dancers in history performed risky and extreme physical moves for the sake of their art. Between the wars were times of great poverty and stress, and the variety dance acts that used tap as their mainstay danced on surfaces that would not be countenanced today, in ways that now seem unnaturally unfair on the body.

At the longed-for top of the tree as a performer, and in a show style such as in *42nd Street*, the dancer will require a tremendous amount of fitness and, it has to be said, not a little youth, either. This example is a young dancer's show, and requires a huge amount of practice and thus stamina not only to get it right, but also so that it is as perfect as possible *and* as precise as possible. Those in their teens and twenties in the chorus dances are fiercely rehearsed, because it is this precision that makes an audience cheer the show to the rafters!

The sheer relentless drilling in this spectacle, and in, say, the show *RiverDance* or *Lord of the Dance*, is what takes such a show, and at the same time a relative of 'tap' dancing, to a whole new level of skill and reputation. This perfect chorus precision is the product of endless rehearsal and practice, and needs a kind of fitness beyond the imagination of the paying public. In these aforementioned shows we see not tap dancing, but a close relation I think you will agree.

FITNESS IN THE HEAD

It is not just the body that dances: it is the brain

and the soul too, and it requires deep concentration and dedication. Dancers – and indeed anyone who uses the body as an instrument to a professional level – will have to be thus dedicated. In sport, the gymnasts and the swimmers and the ice skaters will all attest to the long hours and the extreme effort sustained through recurring injury – and they will all swear that they love to do it! What is it about the human spirit that can suffer, literally suffer, for its art? What makes a person keep coming back for more after a day of intense training, or competition, or performance? What about performers who perform *with injuries* because the show, as we all have heard, must go on?

In the amateur or hobby world of dance, what happens to the person coming along to the class for the very first time? That can be as daunting as coming along to an advanced class for the first time, because the newcomer to the class is not necessarily arriving with lots of other newcomers – rather they are coming along to a class that is in progress already, and yet it is still called 'beginner' level. Well, here we are talking about what I call *fitness in the head*, for want of a better expression. The beginner, or fresh starter, will need to have the sort of brain that relishes the challenge and the prospect of incessant practice, and at first of disappointment. As I have mentioned before, it is aptitude that will get you further.

FITNESS AND THE TYPE OF DANCE

People are all at different fitness peaks and troughs, and some will have problems just with the initial but vital aspect called *balance*. To be able to hold balance on one leg whilst the other is doing something else may seem easy, but not everyone can achieve even this rudimentary stance.

Weight forward and up on the toes – a great way to shapely legs.

Weight forward and moving fast together in a dance lends a dynamic quality to a performance.

I have attended dance classes for the blind as part of a study for my master's degree in perform-ance art, and have seen for myself that that is indeed a challenge. Just to ask for a person without sight to stand 'in parallel' (a basic instruction to anyone wanting to dance on any level, requiring the feet to be in parallel *when looking down* at them) is a minor challenge that a sighted person will not have to face.

To be fit in dance will relate to the kind of dancing being studied. For ballet, a certain amount will have to be a 'given', such as balance, spatial awareness, and a flexible body and a head for detail in coordi-nation; at the intense professional level the correct proportions are also a requirement. Arms and legs in ballet are used in a certain and very specialized way. In jazz, too, the whole body will need to be conditioned and worked on in order to do certain moves.

In, say, a hip hop, or what is often described as a 'street dance'-style class, fitness is not about the body so much as the brain. In this sort of style, flexibility or spatial awareness are not as much a

requirement as attitude. The visual component is more important and this style can be approximated and still look good and effective. The dancer learn-ing a street style may actually want to look as normal as possible, and the *effect* is everything. Fitness can be of secondary importance. I have to admit it is the same in tap in many respects, and as it happens, tap and street dance are both *of the street*! You can approximate ballet and jazz and street, but that is not the way with tap dance, where every single beat must be accounted for and perfectly placed on the rhythm, and where you must also take care to combine the visual aspects.

Approximation in tap is not the way to success, because what is being attempted is extreme detail in sound as well as look, and it is this 'double trou-ble' that often puts off the beginner. It is so detailed and demanding that they can give up early because it is thought to be too difficult. This is what I mean here by 'fitness in the head', or an aptitude for learn-ing the subject, and it is more than likely a natural thing that the person discovers for him- or herself after a few classes. I would say the word 'resilience' is what is needed for tap dance, and that is a part of fitness.

The physical fitness required for tap classes does, of course, matter. The person will need to work on extreme coordination, literally from head to toe, and this attribute alone relies on 'fitness'. Some tap styles are very physical, and jump around in a great many aerial steps, such as pick-ups and wings and turning steps. There are some elevated steps in tap, and also some very fast travelling steps. After the basic elements are mastered, such as shuffles and paddles and tap steps, comes the act of actually *dancing* them, which is another aspect of so-called 'brain fitness' coming into play. This 'dance quality' can be learned, and the good teacher will know how to teach it. An innate feeling for dance isn't necessarily to do with fitness, but rather a fitness for purpose.

PHYSICAL FITNESS REQUIREMENTS FOR TAP DANCING

So what are the normally accepted physical fitness requirements for tap dancing? As this dance style will at some point need to be at speed, the body and feet will have to be trained to move very fast, and faster than the person realizes at first. Constant practice will always improve speed, and this is true of many things we learn in life, such as driving or using a keyboard. Familiarity with the subject, and developing the skills we have learned by being so, are obvious roads to speed. The beginner will perhaps wonder how they can become so fast, and as fast as the teacher, especially as at first they seem to be going so slowly in comparison.

Tap dance is easier to do as a child because children know little about tiredness. Ask any adult to try to keep up with a youth in any sport or game, and they will all have the same reservations. Later, though, the age of the person becomes the key component to learning. So is this fitness? Of course it is! The body learning how to conserve energy and plan moves is the more capable and the more aware, and this is, I believe, a kind of fitness, though

not immediately what some would call 'being fit'. Being aerobically fit is one thing, and steadfastness is another; power is one thing, and resilience is another. All are markers of fitness, and in dance this is evident on many levels.

Maturity and experience themselves are teachers of the body, and also help protect it against the risk of injury: but they are factors that are often not even considered by younger people. The experienced dancer will know what to do to avoid risks, and will be prepared to compromise. A good example is the meeting of two male tap dancers, one who was adept at doing wings, whilst the other did not consider this step important enough to risk putting his knees under such stress. The former dancer ended up with knees that moved in the joint *sideways*, and not as a hinge moving forwards and backwards, in the usual way!

In general, tap dancing can be learned from any age or background, but some things are common to all abilities. The learner will need to know if they are at risk of a back injury because of their own particular situation with their back, or have knee problems, or are prone to dizziness – and so on. Adults will need to be physically active in other ways too, such as walking, or running, or in a job that includes stairs or travelling. Too much of a desk working life can be stressful already on the back and neck, for example. Styles that require nimbleness and light-footed moves are for those people who have a natural energy and life force; however, some people are without this willingness to elevate and give out energy, and perhaps for them it would be better to learn the more 'rhythm tap' style.

FITNESS EXERCISES

Fitness for a normal adult tap-dance class has to do with the following, and of course will involve the ankles, feet and knees especially, but also the rest of the body in some way. Look to do the following: warm up the ankles, the feet – especially in winter when they have entered the studio just minutes before – the knees, the arms, and the torso or middle. A series of exercises can be drawn up for all of these.

The Ankles

Fitness in the ankles is essential since, contrary to some teachings, they are *not* relaxed! They are instead *working*, and as such need to be encouraged to respond to instructions in, say, doing shuffles – and that cannot be done if they are relaxed. What some teachers mean is that they should be flexible, and this of course needs the warming-up period before beginning. Especially with 'wings', where the ankles are at risk of strain on the outward motion, the warm-up is essential. Ankle circles, points and flexes, shaking out and light springing are the best exercises to do to warm up the ankles. Stretching also helps here.

The Feet

The feet themselves are often neglected in tap dance, because for some, jumping is what matters most, and they believe that this is only to do with the knees. Jumping is about the knees, of course, but it is also about the feet, which must be conditioned to taking weight, but *under control*.

For example, when doing a 'ball heel' it is no use just plopping down the ball, then letting the heel fall afterwards in a desultory fashion: in fact ball heels require a sustained and controlled action rather akin to pressing the foot into the floor in a rigid sort of way, followed by a strong heel beat into the floor. The feet need to be strong to do this, and exercises for the arches and the Achilles tendon are important. The dancer always extends the foot fully at the end of the spring in order to get the maximum lift from the floor.

Calf stretches, where the dancer stands up straight, puts the toe behind on the floor and pushes the heel down until it touches the floor, are excellent for this. Injuries such as *plantar fasciitis* are avoidable, and can be relieved by doing calf stretches before and after class. There are people who tend towards cramp in the calves, but stretching will avoid this happening.

The Knees

The knees are very important and are subject to an

Busy legs and feet in a typical tap dance class.

amazing array of injuries. However, if the body in sport has been treated with appropriate care and attention from a player's schooldays, the chances are that they will last a lifetime. If, on the other hand, a young rugby or football player has no regard for injuries that might happen through carelessness in the rough and tumble of the playing field, then as an adult wanting to learn to tap dance he might well have concerns when performing jumps or travelling steps. Knee twists from turns are common, and for dancers they are just a fact of life. In normal life they are perhaps avoidable – though in running for a bus they are a possibility.

The Legs

The legs should be gently exercised by bending and flexing up and down on the spot in the dance studio; furthermore this will obviously incur movement in the feet and ankles as well as the knees. This sort of warm-up is a good preparation for springing and hopping, gently at first, then more vigorously. Such elevated movement involves the lower back and the buttocks, and if all is done in alignment there should be no problem.

However, if this stage hurts the adult learner, he or she should consider whether tap dancing is really for them, or if they need to see a physiotherapist. Springing from one foot to the other generally requires only a low level of elevation, but if the person exceeds a certain weight or has a less than athletic body shape, they will need to think whether this choice of dance is really suitable for them.

The dance styles such as rhythm tap or a smoother jazz tap don't usually involve much jumping, and some people may think this suits them better as a style. To stay a bit more 'grounded' is generally the more preferred state for most adults in a tap class – usually only children love bouncing! Nevertheless these open classes contain people of all ages and all fitness levels, and a teacher should never discourage anyone because of their size. The adult person will soon get to know what is required of their own body, and can decide what is best for them to do.

In other class types, such as show or swing-style

tap, the learner will have to be suitably fit to cope with the jumping and springing and hopping. An energetic style is not for everybody, and especially for older people, say of fifty-five and over. This is a random figure, but is actually quite young compared to some of the class members I teach, proving that in reality age is no real indicator of talent in this dance style. Thus to speak of what is best for what age is largely a *non sequitur*, though sometimes it does have some bearing.

Torso, Hips, Shoulders, Arms, Hands

These body parts can all be utilized in tap dancing. Some classes are more dance-based than others, while some involve more rhythm or footwork – and the serious learner will attempt to do them all. Usually one style is favoured, but an overall strategy is probably the best: for example, swing dancers tend to learn various styles because all have differing steps and moves, but all are classed as swing style.

Standing on both feet, circle the hips and circle the shoulders. The hands are best shaken out and flexed and released. The famous choreographer Bob Fosse invented his own particular and renowned dancing style using the shoulders, hands, head and arms; it has survived long after his death in the late 1980s, and is still popular in professional dance academies today with both younger and older students. Fosse was a tap dancer first and foremost and undoubtedly this gave him a certain poise and a presence that served him in his career. It is interesting to know that another individual stylist called Michael Jackson was also a good tapper in his youth. A tap style is *the* dance style of choice in this book!

BEING FIT TO DANCE

By now we should have realized that to tap dance we need some aptitude and a general fitness, a feel for movement and rhythm, and a love of music, and furthermore that we are not too shy to express ourselves in a studio full of people of all ages. We should also like to make a noise and enjoy the sound we make. This last is not always the easiest because of the practice required, and because the results at first are less than pleasing. But as with any instrument, it has to begin with very basic ideas and elements, and in the early stages will not look or sound like anything you might imagine.

For the advanced tapper who has already acquired ability and expertise the following could be useful:

- gym work for the legs and arms
- exercises for the back, but more especially the knees, now that the tapper has been dancing for a longer time than the amateur
- exercises to get the tapper into the air and on to the toe tips
- work on the wing and pick-up aspects to avoid ankle strain, such as calf raises and knee flexes on leg extension machines
- exercises for speed and agility, since modern tap has a lot of other dance styles contained within it (though not so much ballet!)
- aerobic workouts
- exercises to increase volume and tone, which require subtle distinctions and attention to detail; the tapper will need to gain huge dexterity and patience

All of this I regard as necessary in order to be *fit to dance*, and not for anything else, such as a sport. Tap dance is a very particular form of dancing, and very few other disciplines require the feet and body to move at such a speed. Even in Irish step dance and Spanish flamenco the feet and ankles behave in different ways to tap – as does the body, too, because in Irish dance the body is tightly controlled and remains in the same position throughout, while in Spanish dancing the upright and held position of the man and the gliding body action of the woman maintain the traditional and overtly historical way of dancing.

Tap is freer in both feet and body, and because of this, a great many more people are learning to do it. Coupled with more opportunity, tap dance is universal in appeal and access, and in almost every little

dance school in the country, tap is on the timetable along with ballet, jazz and singing.

As for actual *training* in tap dance, as the saying goes, 'there is no substitute for practice'. This is the only really essential thing in the tap dancer's armoury: the desire to practise, and constantly if necessary. The serious dancer will avidly seek out expert workshops and attend advanced classes in this dance style. Many countries will invite visiting guest artists and teachers, and not only the USA but England, Spain, France and Germany too, and the guest artist is usually American, since America is still the home of great tap.

There is also a very big scene in Australia and Japan, proving that this overtly Westernized dance appeals everywhere where there is, or has been, some jazz music. By contrast I have found that tap dance is not popular in Greece or in such places as Egypt or India, and this must be because the music that is mainly found in those countries does not have a traditional connection to jazz, whereas in London in the 1950s, for instance, and even further back to the 1920s and 1930s, there were jazz singers and dancers and tap dancers in night clubs, theatres and shows. So is there any difference in the styles found in these different countries? Is there such a thing as 'German tap', or 'Australian tap', and does the culture of these places have a bearing on the way it is danced?

It may be to do with the attitude and the energy of the people there: thus vibrant societies such as America and Australia will, I think, do things their own way, so tap might be labelled the 'Australian way', with an overly aggressive or positive set of steps and moves. I was in Australia years ago, and was surprised to find that executing wings was a basic warming-up step! Well, certainly in the class I was attending that day. As for the fitness aspect in that class, in that country, I would say it was very much relevant.

Turning round the whole question of fitness to tap, how about the statement in reverse: 'Will tap dance, or even just dancing itself, make you fit?' In his book *Modern Ballroom Dancing*, the iconic Victor Sylvester wrote:

Ballroom dancing is the most popular pastime in the world. There has been no more striking development in social habits than the rise of dancing to universal popularity. Dancing is a social asset, and for exercise and slimming it is one of the healthiest activities. However little you may know about correct methods of dancing you are sure to be able to pick out of a crowd those who are really enjoying 'dancing' and not merely each other's company; they may not utter a single word during an entire dance, and yet they are really happy.

Victor Sylvester had it absolutely right.

At a basic level tap dance is probably a more enjoyable way to get fit because it does not rely on machines or weights and running machines. It is less laborious and has an earlier result in that, being a creative practice, the results are immediate. Work in the gym will not produce evidence for weeks or even months, no matter what exercises are done. Also, in a public place such as a gym, issues to do with weight or appearance matter, whereas in the tap dance studio they are very low down the worry list.

MUSIC, FITNESS AND ENJOYMENT

Tap dance allies itself with many other important things such as nostalgia and personal history; for some people this is perhaps to do with being a child and learning to dance, and with all that that once entailed in their past. For an older person the music of great singers and bands that they knew when they were young becomes once again relevant in a tap class, and their smile betrays their appreciation of the teacher's informed choice. For them, it becomes a real pleasure to dance to one of their favourite tunes, since in their past they maybe would never have danced to a piece, but only listened.

Now, in this new environment called a tap class, the music can stir memories and feelings connected to past times that they will want to return to again and again. The good teacher in most open tap classes is sympathetic to the student, and will be quite happy to let people muddle along at the back if that is what they want to do. There will be no judgement and only mild pressure from these teachers.

The music could be from a film or from the old Hollywood days that they love, with songs from such artists as Fred Astaire, Gene Kelly and Debbie Reynolds. The music, if chosen correctly by the teacher, will help move their feet and cajole them into going beyond just standing and listening. Keying into our past is important for many people from all walks of life, and songs, music and dance as the creative arts that connect us can truly help us live a better life; 'to dance is to live' as the adage goes.

I would not want the reader to think that tap dance is for the older person; far from it! Today, tap is alive and literally kicking its way to the top again, and this time amongst the energetic younger and older teens. Music is again playing its part, and now it is possible to hear retro sounds and references in a great deal of popular material. Tried and tested rhythmic exchanges and patterns are being used in modern pop songs, and the newer percussive base of modern music gives a distinct advantage to learning to tap dance. In the film *All That Jazz* there is a song with the title 'Everything Old is New Again', and I still use it when teaching professional students, to reiterate that in musical theatre the expressions 'old' and 'new' are meaningless – everything is of value.

A new treatment by a young band of an old classic is often fabulous to hear. Couple this with the fitness aspect that some young people want to get into, and once again the result is enjoyment. Even the fashion angle can be used, and dance wear for today's young girl or boy caters for up-to-date tastes, as demonstrated by fashion brands such as Pineapple, based in London. Strangely, shoes for tap have sometimes not kept pace with younger tastes, but all that is changing, with new colours and new soles producing newer sounds and contributing to tap's continuing success.

So does tap dance make you fit, and can it keep you fit? I would say most certainly it does, and that once you can tear yourself away from the gym, you may not want to go back to it as your fitness 'fix'. Fitness is a happy by-product of tap dancing, and is more accessible to the unfit; in some styles, it is a gentle way to achieve success in terms of fitness. To the tapper of a certain age the tap class in the local school once or twice a week carries real meaning: there is a sense of achievement, and for the amateur to go on and possibly do the occasional perform-ance in whatever capacity, is a sort of crowning glory. Certainly they will have to be fitter to take on this sort of commitment, but that's a good motiva-tor!

So will dancing make you a nicer person? It is well documented that music can make a difference to a person's entire psyche, and studies have shown that it also 'soothes the savage breast'. Is that true, I wonder? And can dance do the same thing? Frank Sinatra is quoted in a biography of Gene Kelly as saying:

More important to me is the creative warmth which Gene generates in the biggest busi-ness of all... daily life. If Gene was endowed with total talent, so too was he endowed with total integrity. Gene climbed to the top, but he didn't step on any hearts on his way up. If they ever get around to handing out Oscars for outstanding performance as a human being, you'll find me on the nominating committee rooting for his buddy Gene.

Now that from a hardened 'pro' about another is praise indeed. In the often cut-throat world of Holly-wood in the so-called golden era of the movie musi-cal it would perhaps have been quite difficult to stay firm as a decent ordinary human being on the way to the top. Kelly had a social conscience by many accounts, and survived on strength of character as well as strength of talent, which is what Mr Sinatra was saying.

Dance made Kelly one of the all-time great personalities and helped the genre to achieve enor-mous international recognition, something he was famously committed to doing in all his films. By his physical presence on film as a fit and likeable guy who just happened to dance beautifully Kelly demonstrated – especially to the male section of society – that to dance as a man in those times was acceptable, both as a pastime and as a career. To do ballet was acceptable and can look just as 'male' as sports. In his television show in the 1950s called *Dancing, A Man's Game*, he invited the current male sports stars in boxing, baseball, American football and athletics to show the similarities used in physi-cal workouts by both dancers and sports stars. This comparison has never been repeated. However, today there is still a certain prejudice against the male dancer.

In recent history dance in some male fraternities was often ridiculed and frowned upon. I can imag-ine the young Kelly brothers on the streets of Penn-sylvania fighting their corner for the right to dance! Especially in those tough times between the wars, it must have taken a strong belief and love of dance just to get yourself to school in one piece. We are all glad that he and others did so.

CHAPTER 9

SHOES AND DANCE WEAR

I have often thought how nice it would be to dance in soft dance shoes and not with taps – not to worry about every single sound and glitch and scrape, knowing that later in some sound studio I could go on and dub the taps! What joy to dance in sneakers or the most fashionable trainers with fabulous designs, and without a care as to what they sounded like because it would all be taken care of!

What speed would be possible, and what carefree moves could be accomplished on a floor that was slippery or hard (or soft), or wet or sticky, or sloping, or worse, uneven? The tap dancer who is capable of doing clever and fast things with feet and brain can be easily defeated and all the rehearsals rendered useless should such conditions face them

NOTE

Tap dubbing is an old Hollywood trick that was entirely necessary because vision with sound was still in the early stages of development – so what you think you are hearing is actually not the real truth. The artist dancers of those times would go into the sound studio separately to dub the taps on after shooting the visual. It was still their sound up there on the screen, but cameras and so on were not equipped to capture perfection; and perfection was exactly what Hollywood was all about.

The 'extras' on some shoes add more excitement, and the options to use the heel and toe are enhanced both by the look and the sound they bring.

A group meeting of like-minded soles.

Shoes on parade, not necessarily in order of merit, but it is easy to see the differences between them.

NOTE

Funnily enough I have danced on the chest of a man supposedly dead on stage with a body cast to take my weight – and with a live dove on my head! I might add I succeeded in keeping that bird from flying off my head whilst I tap danced for more than six minutes! The business of being a professional dancer forever surprises.

in a performance. He or she could be consigned to concrete if the venue were an outdoor event but had a substandard or too small a floor. I have danced on marble, and even on glass with my own tap dance company, and found the experience both unusual and terrifying. It is not so much the shoes that need to be right: rather it is the surface they are going to be working on.

For a great many years shoes for tap were very basic, and were like the shoes a nurse would wear, chosen for their hard-wearing properties. It used to be that whatever the costume, the shoe was always the same! However, nowadays the learner will treasure the moment he buys his first tap shoes – and it is also a love affair for the advanced tapper who has found *the ones* that will propel him to great heights and impress everyone who is watching. Yes, it is possible to be in love with one's tap shoes, at least at first – and even when they are getting old and worn, they are still loved. It is an interesting relationship!

CHOOSING YOUR SHOES

In England there are several makes of dance shoe, and in Europe there are many more. In the USA there are so many styles and makes it would take a proper visit to find that magic pair. Certainly the advanced dancer will want that level of sophistication, but a good working shoe for class work is the Oxford-style shoe, which is sought by both male and female dancer. Ladies still do prefer shoes with heels and ankle straps for some occasions such as a performance, but in general the Oxford shoe, and even better the Oxford shoe with a built-up sole and heavy weighted heel, is the one preferred by many people. But there are more makes than ever on the market nowadays, and the choice is wide enough to suit every taste.

The good teacher in a class will not recommend a particular shoe, but will say that several should be tried before buying, and that some are more useful than others. This is because they can be expensive, and really the beginner should be sure he is going to tap for a long period, rather than just on a whim. Students should try the class and the teacher first, and the studio too, to see if they are going to like tap dance; the beginner can sometimes be discouraged if they feel they are struggling, and this is not uncommon.

A tap shoe must be tried on, in the same way as a suit or a dress, though the main difference is that they are functional above all else. The old makes of shoe, no longer in fashion in England, were made by Annello & Davide and Gamba, and came with or without taps on toes or heels. Other shoe makes, such as Freed or Gandolfi, are still around and remain a good standard shoe. However, back in the early 1980s, the shoes were in need of a revolution

NOTE

Tap almost died completely between the 1950s and the 1970s, and only began its resurgence in the mid- to late 1970s, and on both sides of the Atlantic. In the USA, the home of tap dancing simply had no need for tap in any shows and only appeared on television shows as a novelty. One of those novelties was John Bubbles as a guest artist, and another had Michael Jackson himself tapping with his brothers The Jackson Five: quite a novelty.

in shape, look and sound, and with the resurgence of tap dancing in these years the Americans developed new shoes and new taps.

In 1980s America, after this new wave started to appear, the show *Tap Dance Kid* was a smash hit on Broadway in New York, starring the actor Alphonso Ribiero. In that show a pair of tap shoes was made in the shape of the latest trend in trainers ('sneakers' in the USA): the show actually put taps on to trainers to update the main character and bring tap itself into the modern day. Some tap dancers in England also tried to adapt this type of shoe, but apart from the great tapper Roy Castle and his trainer tap shoes, the idea never caught on. It was a matter of getting the screws for the taps to stay in the rubber sole of the shoe, which is next to impossible. Trainers are by design made with a rubber or soft sole, which is exactly what a tap shoe does not need.

For the record, I have an idea that could bring back that particular feature for the young tappers of today. The toe tap needs to be screwed on to a metal plate within the front part of the shoe and *through* the rubber so that the screw grips the plate and not the rubber. The plate needs to be the same shape and size as the toe tap, and the screws for this must be fairly flat, or they will protrude into the toes! An inner sole inside the shoe protects the toes, should this happen. The heel is even more difficult, but I am sure it can be done.

Normally, however, the taps need to be fixed into a hard leather sole, though many of today's shoes have a composite material sole, which will not hold the screws for long. Tap shoes are for banging, after all, and they have to be tough. Taps will commonly fall off if the shoe has this sort of non-leather sole, so ideally the first tap shoe needs to be an all-leather

Toe 'clips' add weight to steps that are straying into a 'clogging' style, which uses the shoes not just with taps, but by banging various parts together.

Taps are now durable, with a shape that helps to produce a distinct sound. There is a tiny space on both heel and toe taps between metal and board, which means the taps hit the hard soundboard and create a 'click' on the toe taps and a 'clunk' on the heels.

shoe for stability, sound and resilience. Tap shoes can become baggy or loose, so it is even more important that they fit, right from the beginning.

Children's shoes are a different matter because they will be temporary and will be changed as the child grows; nor do they have to be 'state of the art'. A good learner shoe in these circumstances would most likely be made of this composite material, and this is perfectly adequate – though the discerning older tapping child will no doubt rapidly become interested in persuading the parents to buy the more expensive variety! This is a good thing, but only once their feet have stopped growing, of course.

THE TAPS

As with the shoes of old, the taps were also perfunctory! When the taps were added in days gone by they were basic in shape, and even more basic-sounding. The worst feature was that they were thick and so sounded quite dull, and they could seriously cut up a wooden floor! Some heels were in the shape of a horseshoe, and at the two ends of this shape were two very sharp points that dug into the floor. The toe taps were made of a heavy aluminium, and both heels and toes had rivets to hold the taps in place, which would sometimes

The famous Capezio taps are rated very highly because of the toning aspect, using the screws and the soundboard under the taps.

stick out. No loosening was available to tone the sounds, and if they came off you needed to know a riveter!

Also around at this time were 'double taps' or 'jingle taps', which had another, smaller piece of metal inside them that was permanently loose, and rattled. They were also referred to as 'cheat taps', and were shamelessly used by some quite famous dancers! They produced a sort of clanging or ringing sound, and allowed for no real clarity.

At the end of the 1970s I discovered taps and shoes that were nothing short of revolutionary:

my teacher had these brand new idea taps on her shoes, and they were the best thing in taps I had ever heard. Made by the American company Capezio in New York, they are called Tele Tone taps, and to quote Capezio directly:

Capezio's Tele Tone taps are world renowned. The metals used in their legendary engineering has been the same for decades. They are durable, with a shape that helps to produce a robust and distinct sound, and are the choice for tappers the world over.

These great taps are convex in shape, and not just flat. More importantly, they came in a box (and six sizes available too!) with screws and tacks. The tacks were for putting on the included soundboard, made of a stiff fibre material, first, before the taps were connected to the shoes with the screws. This, together with the convex shape, created a tiny space on both heel and toe taps between metal and board, which was to be amazingly useful to every tapper since that time – in a way, rather like the tiny gap in castanets.

This means that the taps do not hit the leather of the sole, but instead hit the hard soundboard and create a 'click' on the toe taps and a darker 'clunk' on the heels, only different in terms of shape. They had the added crucial bonus that the screws were for the specific intention of *tuning* the taps, which meant that *tonality* was finally possible. Capezio

taps are still the taps of choice, or their equivalent from other manufacturers who used the idea!

This tiny gap between the metal and the soundboard was nothing less than astounding, and from that time onwards, the old taps with their rivets became much less popular. Learner shoes for children come with the taps riveted in place, but they serve a useful purpose and have a competent sound quality. These shoes are best with rivets with a view to the safety aspect alone: it is not a good idea to have sharp screws flying about the floor after coming off!

The shoes have also gone through changes. The old English styles are still around, but there are now other makes, such as Capezio, Bloch, Sansha, Leos, and many more. The younger professional of today will have decided on a particular make and style, but even this aspect goes through changes.

The type of shoe chosen should match the style of tap dance being followed.

Shoes that seem to be bursting to dance! The freneticism that advanced tap dancing needs is captured in a restless release of raw energy.

For instance, shoes were once required by dancers to be light, but now the style in fashion is for more weighted soles, and in colours too. Some toes are built up to triple thickness and give a good wallop when the dancer is used to them.

Because the shoes do much of the sound work for the dancer, he has more time to gain in confidence and create richer sounds – providing he is good enough to master the weight. Also the shoe chosen will match the style being followed. This heavier shoe will suit the rhythm tapper ideally. Usually in black, they can be found in plain leather or in a brogue style with hints of trainer in the stitching.

The unisex shoe is the favourite in tap classes, but once in a while the heeled variety of, say, 8cm and in beige with straps, is wanted to make the female dancer look more feminine. After all, the shoe is also a fashion statement, and if performing, the female partner will want this style: the Oxford will definitely not go with a flowing dress and a ballroom type of dance routine. But shoes of this type are harder to master, and ladies can have problems with the high heels and the smaller taps, which can be slippery because they are now perhaps just 2cm of steel and can easily slide about on a wooden floor. Tapping in the Hollywood era must have been excruciating for the women, and I am reminded of the quote about Ginger Rogers who 'did everything Astaire did, but backwards *and in heels*!'

It is also about the ankle flexing. In a high heel the foot is already in a pointed position, so the ankle is restricted for the flexibility that is required: it

The lighter lady's shoe can be difficult to master for some, due to its lack of weight and the exposure to complex work with little ankle support. These are an acquired taste without doubt, and should only be worn when confidence is high.

needs to swivel about a great deal to get the sounds out. This type of shoe for tapping should only be attempted if there is confidence in the technique already, as it can make all the difference between a stilted and an assured performance. The best tap shoes enhance the dancer and look as if they are part of him or her: they allow freedom and have a crisp and lovely sound, so it is difficult to ignore the sound that's being produced.

CLOTHING AND DANCE WEAR

Clothing and dance wear comprise a huge industry, and with the cross-over from the fashion industry it makes for a myriad of choices for the female tapper. I specify 'female', because 'dance' means different things to the man and to the woman in tap classes. Generally speaking for the female their appearance

is quite important, whereas men tend to be more relaxed about what they look like, preferring instead just to make the noise. Really, the man is content with regulation top and trousers, whereas women tend to define themselves by what they wear, and it definitely has an effect on their efforts in the dance studio. Personally, I believe a person works better if dressed for the task in hand: playing tennis in white, swimming in a costume and playing football in a strip brings out a purpose in the game being played.

Having said this, and accepting that even on a basic level taps would be an advantage in a tap class (or even shoes of leather), some will come to a beginner class wearing quite inappropriate footwear – trainers or soft beach shoes, 'thong'-style shoes, wellington boots – even socks and ballet slippers! Shoes are important, and so is dance wear. Thus for the adult female tapper, clothing should be loose

A blend of tap and ballroom is a perfect way to use style of a traditional kind, with music from the big band era but with modern choreography.

and cool – not made of wool, and not leotard and tights, which are strictly for children, and not at all for boys unless really very young. Boys dressed in top and trousers are fine, and girls the same when older. Tap dance and leotard and tights simply don't belong together inasmuch as tap is a jazz dance, and clothing that befits a ballet class will surely be at odds with the idea of jazz.

In an adult class the choice is infinitely personal, and as long as the person can move about unrestricted, anything is allowed. However, jeans, for example, are not a good idea because they can be restrictive – even when the dancer is doing his utmost to be 'cool' in a rhythm tap class with all its attendant attitude. For men in a class the top can be a shirt or a T-shirt, and normal everyday trousers are actually quite the best – tracksuit bottoms will look baggy and saggy, while leggings on a man could be too tight, and with tap shoes on, the feet and legs look like Ls!

For women in a class or studio, what to wear becomes fairly important. In the Pineapple range of dance clothing, for instance, there is a great selection of garments that do indeed cross the line of sport and fashion successfully. The discerning student will feel good when looking good, and this all helps fulfil the maxim of 'dress for the occasion', which aids the effort; it can even be a skirt and leggings underneath for women. This is hardly a new idea, since tap dance on film almost always had women in a skirt or a dress; even today, anything else for ballroom or Latin dancing would not be suitable, and a tracksuit would be quite inappropriate.

Tap can also lead to your body becoming warm and glowing, so beware of tight-fitting garments with a high neck. Sweating is quite permissible in tap, and even encouraged, since it's a great way to detox and allow natural weight loss. Also important is the social aspect. It is a mystery to me why these days – 2017 – there are almost no men in dance classes, especially since tap is certainly a class for both sexes. Perhaps men just don't like the idea of learning something they will struggle with mentally – maybe they think it's just not macho enough. But I also believe this is a very restricting attitude to life.

Tap dancing is historically a 'man's dance', designed I think to express the drumming in the soul and the loud expression of the psyche. Maybe it's a way of letting the world know we are around! The men who do tap classes are often individualists who like to do something out of the ordinary: to get in touch with your dancing soul is quite possibly one of the best things to do in our existence. Furthermore

music has become essential to our well-being, and is the sort of uplifting experience we dismiss at our peril. To *dance* to music is even more uplifting.

Women who tap dance, or who dance in classes, are much better at its social ramifications. The tap class is the meeting point for the lunch or drink that follows. Many friendships are formed in dance classes, which can go on to outweigh the activity, and this is such a great thing to happen. Link this to looking good for our own sake and for others, and tap-dancing class becomes much more than an activity producing noise from the shoes.

Maybe what Isolde said is true, that rhythm is responsible for feelings of friendship and even love, or as she called it, 'romance' – what it can do *for* you, and to you, and how it makes the body feel when it is in tune with the rhythm: magical.

CONCLUSION

If I were to give just one word of advice to the reader who may be thinking of learning to tap dance, it would be the word *listen*: listen to the beat in everything, to the rhythm in everything, to the music in your life and in your inner soul. If you like the thought of learning to do anything, you will already be on the road to doing it. Tap dancing is like that because at first it intrigues, then it turns into an 'I wonder if...', then into an enquiry on the internet, and finally into the act of going along to a class. Maybe you always thought about trying, but you weren't sure how you would go about starting, or whether you would look silly at your age.

It is not a children's activity but an activity for all people of all ages; all people of all ages *with rhythm*. As in the song by Cy Coleman and Betty Comden, who wrote the musical *Sweet Charity*:

> *And the rhythm of life is a powerful beat*
> *Puts a rhythm in your fingers and a rhythm in*
> *your feet*

If, however, you are just intrigued and it stops there, I hope at least to have started something in your head. Even if you don't take up tap, I hope you have had some moments of amusement in reading this book. It was always my intention to introduce you, the reader, to something that I believe is a natural kind of exercise for both body and brain.

Tap dance will enliven you in many ways. In fitness, balance, posture, aerobically, in confidence and in life actually, as you dance alongside lots of other interested people in classes that you attend. Tap dancing is not just for the young, and in fact it is best for the older person, who by then has an inkling of the meaning of that word 'rhythm'. Dance and tap dance can rejuvenate, it can rekindle past memories connected to music, and more especially if that music was merely listened to in the past: now it's possible to dance to it as well. It can revive stiffening limbs and give a feeling of accomplishment, happiness and even joy. Because the body is being used *as the instrument* the dancer feels totally at one with the rhythm, unlike with some modern-day music, with its electronic base.

The electronic beat is not the human beat, rather, it is a falsified invention and is obviously produced by a machine. Music of the past, even the recent past, was produced by human hand, heart, mind and soul. Music produced by artificial intelligence is exactly that, artificial, and cannot touch the soul as it does when produced by a person.

A groundswell of interest in the old musical began in 1976, when the film retrospective *That's Entertainment* was made in Hollywood, starring many of the great artists still alive, and now introducing whole sections in the film on dance and on the musical itself. Gene Kelly, Fred Astaire and Cyd Charisse even came to London on a promotional tour, and interest in tap dance came with them. The jazz 'feel' came retro-like into the late 1970s and early 1980s, and culminated in the theatre-based film with music called *FAME*, which crashed into all our lives in 1980. Music to *dance* to returned with this film, and tap dance was a part of what became a full-blown dance revolution in the 1980s in the UK and elsewhere. The 4/4 rhythm base in all its forms was there, leading the way. In the centres it was 'jazz dance' that was all the rage, with every class full to bursting.

Tap was due a revival, and just a few of us were there at the right time and place to pick up the baton and move forwards. Sometimes I couldn't accommodate any more people in a class because the rooms weren't big enough, such was the interest in the great dance revival. Exercise and aerobics classes led by famous names such as Jane Fonda became hugely popular as well as inspirational. These times were a return to the self, and tap dance is truly about the self, as an instrument, a dance, and a personal quest.

At this time, the current dance centres were opened and are still open in many cities around the world. Before, there were only small jazz clubs, ballrooms and hotel dance floors with small dance bands playing in them. Both tap dance and the jazz dance of those days took off, with seemingly everybody wanting to 'get in on' the new craze of dance.

Tapping to music by Michael Jackson (a talented tap dancer) keeps the genre up to date and relevant.

Fitness through dance also suddenly became hugely popular, with aerobics classes and worldwide book sales by famous film stars, and which is still a phenomenon as popular today as in the 1980s, with the current crop of celebrities; not dance, as such, but of course inextricably linked. Today, wartime nostalgia has made swing music very popular, with thousands of followers dancing at hundreds of events in many areas of the UK.

I believe therefore, that the future of tap dance lies in its relation to its past, and that people learn to do it because of the nostalgic connotations that are so strong in most of us. Tap's flexibility to adapt to almost any music will always see it survive, and fusing tap with ballet and with current jazz modes of dance such as hip hop could produce untold variations. The shows *RiverDance* and the Australian *Tap Dogs* jumped on to the tap scene too in the 1990s, with their overtly ironic connections to folklore and to the industrial work setting! These, however, are now some twenty years old themselves, and are not 'the future' any more; so what about the future?

As I write, some filmed musicals are making their way on to the live stage: *42nd St*, *Singing in the Rain* and the great *Top Hat* are again in our lives. These productions are now really quite old, but the audience is not: they are young, and even the older members are young again for seeing them. Dance does not age, it just comes back, but with a twist. That is the true nature and legacy of this dance called TAP.

FURTHER READING

Buffalino, B. *Tapping the Source: Tap Dance Stories, Theories and Practice* (USA, Cod Hill, 2004).

Feldman, A. *Inside Tap* (USA, Princeton Book Co., Dance Horizon).

Glover, S. *Savion! My Life in Tap* (USA, Morrow & Co. Inc., 2000).

Gray, A. *The Souls of Your Feet* (USA, Grand Weavers, 1988).

(*See also* Bibliography.)

BIBLIOGRAPHY

Ames, G., Siegelman, J. *The Book of Tap* (USA, McKay, 1977).

Astaire, F. *Steps in Time* (London, Heinemann, 1959).

De Mille, A. *The Book of the Dance* (New York, Golden Press, 1963).

Frank, R. E. *Tap! The Greatest Tap Dance Stars and their Stories* (USA, De Capo, 1990).

Gorer, G. *Africa Dances* (Lehmann, 1949).

Hartley, D. *Teach Yourself Tap Dancing* (London, Hodder ed., 2007).

Hirschhorn, C. *Gene Kelly* (London, W. H. Allen, 1974).

Isolde *Tap-Dancing Made Easy* (C. A. Pearson, circa 1936).

Stearns, M. and J. *Jazz Dance: The Story of American Vernacular Dance* (USA, Schirmer Books, 1968).

Sylvester, V. *Modern Ballroom Dancing* (London, Jenkins, 1952).

Wade, R. *Tap Dancing in Twelve Easy Lessons* (England, Foulsham, circa 1936).

ACKNOWLEDGEMENTS

Thanking the many thousands of people who have enriched my life since I began dancing so long ago would take some time and would revive some heartfelt moments. The people who turn up at tap dance classes often fall into the category of eccentric, but I have always been completely all right with that, and think that it's all part of this wonderful and crazy dance. Certainly my own teacher looked crazy and fierce, and I think all tappers are slightly peculiar to want to do it obsessively! It has to be the rhythm – as Gershwin said, it can drive one crazy.

First I want to thank my parents, who understood far ahead of their times that a man can have dance as a career, and that this can be perfectly normal. This was in the late 1960s, and they were simply full of encouragement and very positive. Another person to recognize is the late Joy Adams, my teacher, who was teaching in London when I was twenty-seven years old. I thought I could tap dance when I went to see her, but it turned out I had to start all over again – which I did, from the very first day.

It is, of course, impossible to think of everyone whom I must thank, and some people have been on this journey alongside for many years: Diane Hampstead, my stalwart proof reader and a major tap dance presence; Debbie Moore from The Pineapple in London; and all the college staff who, over so many years and from all the major places of learning in the UK, are either still around or have 'left the studio'.

For my photographs I want to thank professional photographer Malcolm Smith especially and Karen King from my classes; and the many studio owners who have welcomed us in to practise our creations. Over the years I have visited many countries in response to invitations to teach workshops and contribute choreographies, and I thank them. Without the never-ending support and patronage of so many people in my London classes I would not be writing this book: I would not have been asked.

I would like to thank my publishers for asking me to write this book – written from the heart, I might add. I would like to thank Claire, my dance partner of the last five years, as we go about the task of dancing as a 'Fred Astaire and Partner' tribute act in venues across the UK, dancing to some wonderful tracks from the era we both love. I can think of no other person who has been able to remember in detail all my myriad musings and teeming tap thoughts so that we could dance together.

I would like to thank all those who have supported our performances, and all those who attend tap classes anywhere, and my tap classes too; also all who have attended my workshops, and all the past students of this dance form who are now working in the business professionally: I would not be where I am without having been pushed to it by great dancers who have come before and after my dance career.

Finally, I would like to thank tap dance: it has been a pleasure to know you.

INDEX

RELATED TITLES FROM CROWOOD

The Art of Illusion
TERRY ACKLAND-SNOW WITH WENDY LAYBOURN
ISBN 978 1 78500 343 1
240 illustrations 192pp

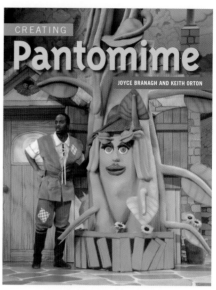

Creating Pantomime
JOYCE BRANAGH AND KEITH ORTON
ISBN 978 1 84797 255 2
180 illustrations 208pp

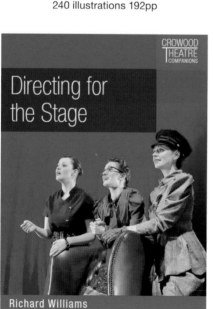

Directing for the Stage
RICHARD WILLIAMS
ISBN 978 1 78500 379 0
60 illustrations 160pp

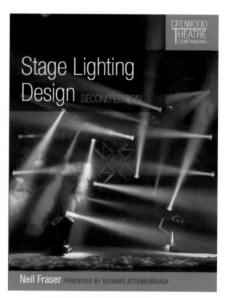

Stage Lighting Design
NEIL FRASER
ISBN 978 1 78500 367 7
150 illustrations 208pp

In case of difficulty ordering, please contact the Sales Office:

The Crowood Press, Ramsbury, Wiltshire SN8 2HR UK

Tel: 44 (0) 1672 520320   enquiries@crowood.com   www.crowood.com